Streaming
Consciousness

Streaming Consciousness

A CURRENT OF UNITY

Louise Platt Hauck

www.louisehauck.com

Lamplight Publishing Company
511 6th Avenue, Ste. 234
New York, NY 10011

Copyright © 2013, 2020 by Louise Platt Hauck.
All rights reserved.

www.louisehauck.com

ISBN 978-0-9769205-7-1

Publisher's Cataloging-in-Publication Data

Hauck, Louise Platt.
    Streaming consciousness: a current of unity / Louise Platt Hauck.
        p. ; cm.
ISBN: 978-0-9769205-2-6
1. Hauck, Louise Platt.   2. . I. Title.

Printed in the United States of America

*Dedicated to the memory and
sweet spirit of John Hughes*

Table of Contents

Acknowledgements

*Feeling gratitude and not
expressing it is like wrapping
a present and not giving it.*

—WILLIAM ARTHUR WARD,
Foundations of Faith

*I*nspiration for my writing has always come, first, from my clients. They ask the questions that prompt the Universe to deliver, through me, a few answers (or at least some new perspectives). Some inspire me by the way they live their lives, struggling through unbelievable circumstances, their faith giving them strength and hope to persevere. Others yearn to have faith in something greater than themselves to believe in, *to surrender to*, or to love more than themselves in order to make wiser choices. Many exhibit great courage in the simple act of staying present long enough to figure things out.

There are seekers who've awakened to their spiritual path and have learned ways to turn stumbling blocks into stepping stones, and those who are simply curious by nature, trying to fit the pieces of this grand puzzle together. Some sense that there must be more to this crazy world, and are searching for new ways to see.

Often, the journey toward truth is a lonely one. Some naturally intuitive clients feel like outsiders, often judged, and even condemned for the way they see or know things. They remind me to give thanks for my own way of seeing things, and for the ongoing confirmation I receive—that those very precious gifts come from God.

Inspiration, particularly for this book, has also come from my beloved apprentices. They're always so enthusiastic about going with me on new multidimensional adventures, and then reporting back with findings from their own further experimentation. A recent bunch is highly intuitive and brings diverse life experiences to the work. Brad is an engineering consultant, Karyn was trained as a microbiologist, and Susie is retiring from a career in mechanical engineering. Our sessions together have provided grist for the mill and allowed me to test out many of the ideas and concepts that have fed *Streaming Consciousness.*

Another group of apprentices were extremely helpful and *unbelievably* patient, finding their way into my online meeting room while I tested video conferencing technology that allows me to conduct online classes. Vanessa Jasper and Mimi Mills assisted me during those trials, sometimes hanging out in noisy coffee shops while I worked through the bugs from the comfort of my office.

Inspiration has also come from those who never cease to believe in me. Jaene Leonard has always done so, ever since we first met at the Markle in New York City. She's a talented actor and writer. So it goes without saying that she's had tremendous focus as my editor. Jaene helps me think in a straight line, when my non-linear, right-brain thinking gets me wandering off in tangential dimensions, bringing me back with the simple but profound question: "What are you trying to say?" This book would not have been possible without Dear Jaene.

Dylan is my son, producer and webmaster. He's very left-brain smart and right-brain creative. He's responsible for whatever bits of computer savvy I employ that enables Illuminations to run efficiently and effectively. Many many years ago, my computer tutorial began with him sitting me down at my new Mac Plus. 'Mom," he said, pointing to the little 5x7 green-ish screen, "think of it as a desktop," he said. Like Jaene, Dylan is also a visionary who has a sense of where I'm going *way before I get there.*

Pat Barrentine, Maryann Novajosky-Bankman, and Laura Roe-Stevens gave the manuscript a combing through, each generously contributing their time and proofreading expertise. A talented media producer came on board to produce the book trailer (a real miracle!) while Greg Ryan and Cynthia Mayfield checked in regularly to cheer me on.

Many thanks to friends and family for all your continued love and support. Where would I be without you?

I am so blessed, most of all, to be so Divinely guided to serve. This work humbles me. For moments in which I'm pulled into the Current of Unity to feel our Oneness, I'm grateful beyond words. For you readers who are willing to stretch, and perhaps challenge some of your own beliefs about things, there's no time like the present!

chapter one

The Stream

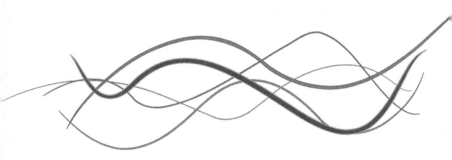

*Human consciousness is just about
the last surviving mystery. A mystery
is a phenomenon that people don't
know how to think about—yet.*

—Daniel C. Dennett,
Consciousness Explained

Imagine an invisible Stream of limitless possibilities. Picture this Stream infused with the spark of spirit. Feel the surge as this spark ignites and moves your soul forward through eternity. Hear the rushing as this Stream flows toward your wildest dreams. And beyond.

This Stream is always there, around you, enveloping you, emanating unconditional love from God and all the manifestations of that infinite energy—among them creativity, inspiration, wisdom and intuition. Within the flow is a magnetism that unites all things, physical and non-physical. We're all One in this Stream.

Streaming Consciousness flows through you whenever you move from fear to love, from head to heart, from thinking to feeling. As you practice this movement, and learn to trust your heart, you will feel yourself nudged forward in the flow in more and more moments, experiencing gentle confirmations, unexpected synchronicities and cosmic winks.

In my work as an intuitive spiritual counselor, I feel as though I'm on duty in a bridge house overlooking various waterways in the Stream. It's my job to help clients find new directions leading toward more fulfilling lives.

All of us, at one time or another, have found ourselves lost in murky waters, becoming mired in the muck, feeling like we're treading water, and at times unable to untangle ourselves from constricting fear or stagnating regret. Past experiences may have left us feeling diminished or compromised, our integrity or self-worth challenged in some way. We forget that free-flowing waters are just around the bend.

We can lose our bearings and find ourselves swept into darkened coves. For a time, we're unable to find our way out. Some eventually do so by seeking guidance, help for addictions, depression, post-traumatic stress, grief or despair, and other challenges. We're all forced to confront our own darkness at some point—it is part of our journey—and we must learn to embrace it. This requires us to take responsibility for our choices and leave blame behind. The wake from each challenge lands us in a new place. This new point of reference helps us refine our values and re-prioritize our goals. It's by doing the difficult work of coming to terms with ourselves that we learn how to ease our way back into the flow of Streaming Consciousness.

The more you become aware of being in this flow, the more you'll begin to see yourself as a timeless soul who is ever evolving and always expanding. You'll discover the soul's ability to observe itself and will gain tremendous insights as you start to view your life from this new perspective. You'll notice how certain, old responses to familiar challenges can spin you into circles of frustration, whereas making the choice to first switch into Observer Mode will free you up and allow you to respond in new ways.

You'll also begin to recognize when you are operating from the imposing Ego-self and use your will to operate in more moments from your Higher-self. As you begin to distinguish between the two and release the Ego-self in difficult moments, old themes will begin to neutralize and repeating patterns will fall away.

In the flow of Streaming Consciousness, you can perceive beyond your life—this subjective and temporal existence—to a much grander plan in play. This expanded way of participating in the unfolding bigger picture will help you maneuver beyond limiting beliefs and perceptions that inhibit and restrict you. By operating more from this new perspective, you will be shaping your *own* future, making your *own* dreams a reality, all while assisting in the evolution of humankind. To join in this revolutionary movement, the first step is to look at your beliefs, allow your perceptions to shift, and to free your imagination.

Belief:

noun—a state or habit of mind in which trust or confidence is placed in some person or thing; something believed; *especially*: a tenet or body of tenets held by a group.

— Merriam-Webster

A belief is something we hold to be true about ourselves, about others, or about the world. Some beliefs have been taught to us. Others are formed as we move through our own experiences. Throughout a lifetime, we collect many beliefs that anchor us to our place in the world around us, and give us a sense of safety and predictability. We define ourselves by our beliefs and cling to them as a way of explaining or justifying ourselves to the world.

Certain mass beliefs exist that make up 'consensus reality.' These are agreed-upon concepts that a particular culture holds collectively to be true. Our Western belief system, supported by mass media, includes the notions that more-is-better, fame-is-greater, and the attainment of money, power or celebrity is the ultimate goal.

These beliefs are illusory, always out of reach, and ultimately unsatisfying. We go through life blindly seeking such goals, unsure as to when (or why) we took them on as our own. The pursuit drives us, but even when fame, money, or power is attained, *the soul still seeks purpose.* We each attach to our own assortment of these illusions, until we finally become *dis*illusioned. Life has a way of showing us, again and again, that all things gained are almost as easily lost.

At these major junctures of disillusionment, our spiritual journey really begins, (or, as the case may be, restarts). We begin to ask the bigger questions— why am I here? What do I need to learn? Once our eyes adjust to the darkness, we begin to see the play of light. We register the difference in our bodies when we experience Truth versus inauthenticity. We notice ourselves expanding when we feel love, and contracting when fear is present. We make the happy discovery that we can *choose* one over the other.

When our beliefs answer these bigger questions and withstand the test of time, we preserve them and persevere with them. We assume that a certain belief will always be true, since it has been true in the past, and because it has served us well. But beliefs can have shelf lives and change over time, and may even be replaced.

A belief falls away when it no longer works for us. An illuminating insight or 'ah-hah' moment may give rise to a new idea that resonates more than an old belief. If this idea continues to hold truth for us, it may become a belief that expands and serves us well—at least for a while.

When we encounter an opposing belief, the Ego-self can feel threatened and defensive. Many folks feel and act as though they're fighting for their lives when they debate issues, clubbing each other over the head with differing beliefs. When you find yourself getting caught up in the divisiveness of today's issues, perhaps feeling polarized or contentious, this might be a signal that you're holding on too tight, and possibly defining yourself by your beliefs.

Holding fervently to rigid beliefs closes you off to new knowledge or a possible blending of ideas. A new consensus can serve the greater good. This is impossible when the Ego-self is running the show.

I know it's my 'Edith Ego' taking control when I hear myself using words like 'never' or 'always'. Things in absolute terms rarely amount to anything more than Edith doing her dance (and she *loves* an audience). When I switch into Observer Mode and note that she may be trying to impose a limiting belief on another, I imagine tucking that belief into my pocket. The instant I do this, I feel an immediate shift.

This little maneuver releases me to be fully present, receptive and ready to listen to another's perspective, no matter how greatly it might differ from my own. I'm left feeling more comfortable with myself, and more in harmony with others. Later, I'll take that belief back out and have a closer look. How does this belief serve me? Does it marginalize others? If the answers are slow in coming or somehow elevate me over others, I'll consider throwing it in the recycling bin.

Allow yourself to release beliefs that you may be holding tightly, ones that contract rather than expand you, or those that may cause you to feel fearful or judgmental of others. Embrace new beliefs that welcome you into the flow of life, and allow you to feel respectful of, and connected to, others. We're traveling along together in the Stream of ever-evolving consciousness. There's room for all.

We can trust beliefs to be ones that truly serve us when we're left with a sense of quietude and peacefulness within ourselves. There's no need to convince anyone of anything. We feel a pleasant stillness.

Perception:
noun—awareness attained directly through any of the senses, especially sight or observation.

—Merriam-Webster

When an old belief falls away, we experience a shift in perception. This shift often triggers a change in our reality. Things look different. We feel different. It may be a little scary. Our impulse may be to fight these changes. If we do, we may feel everything's against us, as though we're treading water or swimming upstream. But if we stay open, life can feel softer and more yielding, even more forgiving. A receptivity to new ideas emerges. Our perceptions are no longer stuck in the foundation of rigid beliefs. We no longer need to see things a certain way in order to validate our beliefs. These moments can lead to profound transformation.

Edith Ego can be very stubborn and convincing in her estimation of people and situations. I have a friend who has always enjoyed telling off-color jokes in my presence—though he knows me well, knows the nature of my work, and knows I find these jokes offensive. Edith and I both believed beyond a doubt that he would be forever stuck in a pattern of acting in this inconsiderate manner. Though I'm not a combative person, Edith always had a string of clever comebacks ready for him. Thankfully, I'm usually successful in resisting the urge to draw from her stockpiled arsenal.

I could feel myself bracing whenever we were going to meet. The last time we met, however, my friend was extremely kind and considerate and seemed to be making a real effort to be inclusive. I was pleasantly surprised. For her part, Edith was shocked and suspicious. She kept waiting for him to show his true colors and had a whole speech ready for when he would.

When I got home, I let Edith run through her rant, *Oh, he was just putting on a show . . . he wasn't being himself . . . he just wanted to impress you . . . don't trust him.* Our egos are rigged to protect us—from being hurt, wrong, betrayed—and to keep us *in the right.* Edith means well, and I let her know I appreciate all she does. I put her gently in time out and switched to Observer Mode.

I could sense that something else was at play. After sitting with it for a while, I realized that the resistance I was feeling, (and retorts that Edith was filling my head with), were all due to a belief that was trying to fall away. My perception of this friend was shifting. This was something I had hoped would come about for a long time. Now that it was quite possibly happening, I was having a hard time letting go of my old ideas about him.

Taking a fresh look at established relationships is always challenging. But people do change, grow, and *awaken.* I owed it to our friendship to let in his sincerity and kindness. And I owed it to myself to allow this evolution of our connection and of my own limited perception of another human being.

I was raised in a family with fairly open-minded parents who embraced the notion that we live in a big world containing varied cultures and differing beliefs. Because we weren't well-traveled, I can't say that we were very worldly.

As kind and fair-minded as my parents were, they still bestowed upon me the inference that there are those in life who are *not like us.* The message was subtle, but it nonetheless implied that those who differed in appearance, lifestyle or beliefs might tend to be less enlightened or perhaps not as smart as people *like us.* Assumptions such as these can become deeply embedded beliefs.

Several years ago, I found myself in an experience that challenged my perceptions and transformed me. I was sitting in a theatre in an urban area of a city I didn't know very well, treating myself to a holiday viewing of *How the Grinch Stole Christmas.* In the dark theatre, I was acutely aware that I was surrounded by a number of what my parents might have called 'tough-looking characters.' Because of leftover familial beliefs, I felt a little anxious.

The movie began. All of a sudden, those I had perceived as tough guys were reciting, *verbatim,* Dr. Seuss' well-known words. My beliefs about people 'like them' swept away, and we were the same. All of our child-selves were enjoying the movie together. As I left the theatre, I saw everyone anew. One really, truly *cannot,* and for the sake of our evolution *must not,* judge a book by its cover.

All my life, I've learned over and over that the surest way into a new group of people or a new community is to find *that which connects us,* rather than separates us. We all seek love, support, and validation. We've all been children and know what it is to dream and imagine. We all know loss, pain, and loneliness. When we connect with each other on these human levels, we move beyond boundaries and into new relationships with each other. These shifts in perception and falling away of stale beliefs nearly always promote in me a change of heart, opening me up again and again to the truth that we are all connected—all One in the Stream.

Allow perceptions to shift and you'll feel a new sense of wonder, curiosity and receptivity. You'll begin to realize there are many different ways of seeing and that there's so much more going on behind the scenes with others than we can *ever* know, (though our Ego-self will usually disagree).

You'll feel a new kind of freedom that releases you from having to be right, smarter or better than anyone else. A change of heart will bring you right back into the flow!

Projection:
noun—the way in which something is regarded, understood, or interpreted.

— Oxford Dictionary

When we think we know *exactly* what's going on with friends, family, or even strangers, we're often imposing our own thoughts, feelings or erroneous assumptions unconsciously onto others. We may judge what we see as some inadequacy in them, or in the way they handle their challenges. We may assume their experience is the same as ours, (or what ours would be, were we in their situation). Or, we may seek to be instructive to them, convinced that we understand more about their situation as an outsider than they do as the experiencer! These are *not* intuitive sensings, even though they may be well-intentioned. These are *our projections.*

I once felt inspired to help a blind person cross the street when I found us arriving at an intersection at the same time. I offered the woman my arm, and she took it graciously. I led the way until we reached the other side of the street, where she used her cane with great expertise to step up onto the curb. Assured that she'd arrived safely, I started to continue on my way. Edith was feeling terrific about being so helpful. To my surprise, the woman reached out and grabbed my arm, pulling me toward her. "Now," she said, let me tell *you* how to assist a blind person!"

"First," she said, "let the person know you're there, but don't assume they need assistance." She smiled. "Many of us are *very* independent."

"When blind people wait at the corner after the light has changed, don't assume that we're waiting for help. We usually listen for traffic noise going in front of us, and then wait for the sound of perpendicular traffic to start so we understand the rhythm of the traffic and know when it's safe to step off the curb."

I felt quite humbled and embarrassed by the encounter, but most certainly enlightened by the woman's instruction. I had obviously projected what I thought *I'd* be feeling or needing in *her* situation. In the end, I felt that I had acted in a presumptuous and intrusive manner. But when we parted, she thanked me for my willingness to reach out.

If you can switch into Observer Mode and take note of how you perceive others, you might also discover hidden judgments or annoyances you carry about yourself, those you've denied or pushed aside. It is *these very issues* with which we must come to terms within ourselves. Otherwise, we will continue to notice, focus on, or even be repelled by these things in others. We must learn to observe these outward projections and use them as reflections of our own unresolved issues.

One day I was puttering around the kitchen while chatting with a friend on the phone. She was expressing concern about having noticed that with each passing year, her behavior was getting increasingly more obsessive. She said she'd become extremely focused on making sure everything was in its place and in proper order. Her signature perfectionist tendencies were starting to run her ragged and drive her family crazy.

"You know," I said to my friend, "one theory says that the more we may be feeling out of control in our lives, the more we might try to control whatever we can in our immediate world, completely unaware that we're doing so!" We talked at length on the matter before ending the call.

I returned the phone to its cradle on the counter, and then turned around. I was stunned at what I saw. Looking back into an open cabinet, I realized that during the entire conversation with my friend, I'd absentmindedly reorganized my entire spice collection, arranging each little jar in alphabetical order! I had to ask myself— *just who is the one feeling the need to create some order in her life?*

As you start to observe your own projections, you will also gain greater acceptance of what you perceive as your own issues and shortcomings. People who seem the most critical of others are often the hardest on themselves. In a sense, they're projecting their own expectations of unattainable perfection or excellence onto others. If you find this to be true for yourself, this insight will hopefully lead you to be more gentle and patient with yourself and others. *We all have work to do.*

Here's a tip: if there's something about another person that really gets under your skin, or an issue that you find yourself being overly attentive to, simply ask yourself, *does this same issue relate directly to me?* You'll be surprised what you can uncover with this simple question. We're all incredibly unique individuals arriving on the scene from diverse backgrounds, different teachings, varied experiences and points of view.

Thought:

noun—the product of mental activity; a single act or product of thinking or reasoning; an idea or notion; a consideration or reflection.

—Dictionary.com

Our mind can become incredibly loud and busy. Sometimes, our brain generates non-stop thoughts that can make us feel fretful, tired and confused. Getting enough rest, physical exercise, and making healthy food choices all do wonders for neutralizing running thoughts, and so does engaging in human contact. When you're really present with someone else, it's more difficult for thoughts to race and drive you into feeling uncomfortable.

It can be more difficult to quiet the mind when we're alone. Our thoughts can take us far away, or trap us in a well-worn story or tired old theme.

When we're alone with our thoughts, they can also lead us to feelings of longing for someone (or something) we feel our lives may be lacking. Switch into Observer Mode and watch where your thoughts take you.

As you practice observing thoughts, you'll begin to see which thoughts serve to evolve you and which ones hinder you. Clues to the value of a thought lie in how it registers in your physical body. Does the thought make you feel good? Does it make you relax? Or does it make you feel tense or anxious?

Feeling powerless or misunderstood in our lives may trigger what I call a *thought loop*. This is a cycle of thoughts that are incessant and intrusive. They're hard to divert and next-to-impossible to quiet. They tend to race and go around and around in our head. This kind of thought loop may be a sign that some change needs to take place—either with our handling of a situation, or the way we're seeing it. Sometimes we need to talk it through.

If the thought loop still seems unstoppable, spend a few moments in silence. We all have a warehouse full of favorite memories. They made us feel something really wonderful when they happened, and they still make us feel the same way when we recall them. Think about what your moments are. Write them down. Whenever you notice that you're replaying a scene over and over in your mind, unable to reach any resolution, recall any one of your favorite moments. Sit with it and allow it to fill you fully. Ground yourself in what really matters. The struggle will pass.

Edith Ego is a pro at pulling me into a thought loop. I realize that she's up to her old tricks when I find myself rehearsing dialogue in my head for future conversations, often in anticipation of getting in my two cents—or setting someone straight. Edith wants to *win*, to be *right*, to have the upper hand. The quicker I observe Edith's Ego-self antics and return to my Higher-self, the sooner the mind quiets and I'm back in the flow. *Down, Edith. Down!*

Thoughts that make me feel expanded and connected, rather than small, defensive, and alone are the ones that move me forward and empower me. These are the thoughts I want to cultivate. Sometimes it's just plain difficult to get to the expansive ones, when negative thought loops keep spinning us around! We can never shut off the mind, but we can use meditation to deepen our understanding and practice switching into Observer Mode.

The benefits of a regular meditation practice are all over the news these days. But the term 'meditation' itself is still difficult for some people to grasp. Meditation is simply a way to corral the mind, which, by its very nature, tends to run rampant from thought to thought to thought.

Buddhist teachings refer to thoughts in the mind as chattering monkeys, each squawking louder to draw our attention. These congested, busy thoughts take us out of the flow in a flash. They need to be observed and quieted to allow guidance and highly intuitive data to flow to us from Streaming Consciousness.

Some kind of meditation is essential for learning how to create space between busy thoughts, and then to *lengthen* that space. This is a case where practice makes perfect. Twenty minutes twice each day is ideal.

Learn about different meditation techniques and find the one that works best for you. Check out books and DVDs online or from the library. Try different approaches to meditation on your own, or guided by a teacher (in person or on a CD). For some, simply counting breaths works to quiet the mind. For others, focusing on an object in nature helps—perhaps a flower or a tree. I learned mantra meditation, in which one repeats a word or phrase over and over to oneself. Eckhart Tolle suggests a great mantra—"All is well . . . all is well."

When you find the meditation technique that fits you, you'll begin to look forward to meditation. Your old excuses about not having enough time to meditate will fall away. (The Universe has a powerful way of configuring things in your life, *beyond time*, whenever you focus intentionally on something wholesome and worthy.)

Here's an easy meditation you can do whenever you observe yourself caught in a thought loop:

Take a deep breath and come into the present moment. Close your eyes if it helps. Imagine you're sitting next to a river. You watch as the river flows. Driftwood in the river floats past. You see it and watch it go by. Then it's gone. Thoughts arise in your awareness. See them as driftwood in the river. You acknowledge them. Then they drift out of your awareness. Observe, acknowledge, let go. By treating them in the same way you observe the driftwood, no single thought leads you to more thoughts. Observe, acknowledge, let go.

Meditation helps us soften around our thoughts, beliefs, perceptions. It helps us practice being present and quieting the mind's natural chatter. The more we familiarize ourselves with these feelings of balance and quietude, the more we begin to sense the subtle difference between simply existing in Streaming Consciousness, and *consciously moving into the flow of it*. In order to manifest all the things we truly desire in life, getting into the flow in more moments (and learning tools to get back into the flow when we've somehow gotten off course) is essential. It is in this flow that we open to the real gifts of Streaming Consciousness.

Left-Brain vs. Right-Brain Thinking

The mind is a place where the soul
goes to hide from the heart.

— MICHAEL SINGER, author
of *The Untethered Soul*

The brain is a marvelous computer that allows us to interact with our physical world. When you are being analytical, attentive, objective and rational, the left side of your brain is activated. This is the part you use to process language, facts, and strategies. It enables you to parse data, leading you to rational conclusions and practical solutions. The left brain stores content and catalogues it in a way that lets us identify certain external stimuli (leaves ... bark ...) and then make necessary associations (leaves + bark = tree). This is how we relate to our material world.

The left brain also serves as a command center, steering our bodies through complex neurological mechanisms as we roam about in this physical reality. It collates data we gather through our five senses and delivers us to necessary, autonomic responses to our environment and, on demand, archived information stored in our memory.

The right brain, on the other hand, offers us the ability to access creative thought concepts—the kind of thoughts that open us to ideas beyond our rational selves and beyond the five senses of physical experience. Creativity, impulsiveness, and intuition are the domains of the right brain, which processes visual impressions and multi-tasks. Feelings and imagination drive the right side.

Right-brain thinking isn't really thinking. It's more feeling, sensing, allowing. Operating from the right side of the brain allows us to ponder and entertain abstract questions, such as—*What is eternity? Who am I? Who (or what) is God?* When life prompts us to ask these questions, and we're ready and open, our own answers begin to trickle through the right brain in the form of inspiration and epiphanies.

Part of your work involves learning which side of your brain is dominant and embracing your particular orientation. Foster a curiosity about your non-dominant side and develop the capacity to switch back and forth between the two.

Generally speaking, a person who operates predominantly from the left brain will navigate to feelings from thoughts, while a person who operates from the right brain will navigate to thoughts from feelings. When I ask left-brain dominant clients how they're feeling, they might first express a thought about the feeling, rather than access the feeling itself. They tend to access certain sentiments as knowable or understandable, but almost *outside of* their own experience.

Right-brain dominants will almost always jump right to feeling, sometimes with excessive passion.

For example, if I ask, "How did you feel when you learned that your partner gambled away your savings? The left-brain dominant client might reply—

"*Well, anyone would feel betrayed . . .* " while the right-brain dominant client might say,

"*I was mad as hell!*"

Right-brain processing is the way into Streaming Consciousness. In readings and workshops with clients who want to tap in and develop their intuition, I try different tactics to help them shift from left- to right-brain thinking. I might ask one to go to the feeling of loving their child or pet, or to try to see something through the eyes of their playful, imaginative child-self. When I'm successful at helping others to make the shift, I can almost hear a discernible—'CLICK!'

With left-brain dominants, I take time to explain that information brought in through right-brain sensing is *subjective* and must be sorted out, in a manner similar to dream interpretation. There are no absolute meanings. This can initially prove frustrating for left-brain dominants. I encourage them to remain open as we explore deeper meanings. As more seasoned left-brained clients become oriented to the process of receiving and interpreting intuitive data, they can show a surprising capacity to organize it into real-world applications. This is putting the left brain to its best use!

Learning to blend left- and right-brain tendencies helps us respond to our life challenges in a myriad of ways. We can all use a little more organization—or a little more spontaneity—in our lives. To offset your habits and left- or right-brain dominance, try doing daily activities with your non-dominant hand. If you are right-handed, use your left hand to write, and vice versa. Try brushing your teeth, combing your hair, or holding the phone with your other hand.

After feeling a nudge to balance out my time at the computer recently, I bought a keyboard with the intention of reviving my piano repertoire from twenty years ago. A half-hour of daily practice is adding delightful contrast to my life. I start with form, which my left brain loves—say for example, Bach—and then I move on to the more lyrical, creative expression that Chopin invites, re-engaging my right-brain. I return to my work feeling refreshed and balanced.

Engaging the Right Brain

Try to shake things up a bit. Take a different route to work. Sit in a different chair. Use a different mug for your morning coffee. Or have tea instead.

Once you train yourself to experience feelings before thoughts, you'll find yourself moving more easily into right-brain thinking. If this seems difficult for you, try this: when something happens and you want to recount it to someone or play it over and over in your head, try instead to locate where you feel the impact *in your body.* Ask yourself "where do I feel this and what does the feeling feel like?" This takes some practice, but over time, you'll find your feelings becoming more and more readily accessible.

One very left-brained apprentice surprised me at the start of a phone session by saying very softly,

"Just a sec. Let me flip that switch . . . "

I asked him if he knew what he'd just said.

"No," he replied, "*what*?"

Receiving validation over time for his lesser-used right-brained intuitive processing had created a pathway from the left brain, linear mode to his right brain, intuitive mode. He'd inadvertantly made the shift.

Paying attention to little details will also help to engage your right brain. Take a few minutes off to switch into Observer Mode at the bus stop shelter where you wait for your bus, or take note of the layout of your car's dashboard. Check out the hardly-noticeable characteristics of your workspace. Close your eyes and try to recall specific details. Doing this regularly will strengthen your Observer Mode skills in the present moment.

Allow yourself to see things within things. Look for images in clouds. See the human face traits on the front (or back) of cars. I can't help but see standout images when I try to nap beneath textured, bumpy ceilings. (It drives me crazy!) Anything creative and improvisational is a right-brained activity: drawing, writing, dancing, acting, gardening, cake decorating, knitting, finger painting, sculpting, folding origami, anything you can do for a sustained amount of time (say, twenty minutes) will get you into the right brain's 'zone.' Think outside the box!

As you start your creative activity, notice the initial left-brain engagement, the constant commenting, the impulse to scrap and start over and do it better, the inner-nagging telling you this is a waste of your time. Visualizing and then immediately implementing is the left brain's forte—point A to point B in a flash. The slow-motion process of any endeavor is the domain of the right brain. You may feel discouraged. Stay with it!

As the mind becomes fully engaged in activity, these play-by-play thoughts and criticisms give way to a full experiencing. Thoughts shift, and the fun begins when you enter the creative mind-space. Natural curiosity and wonder replace a need to control the outcome.

My family has always shown both right- and left-brain tendencies. My father was an aeronautical engineer who used much of his free time designing and implementing creative improvements to our home. My mother was a pianist who graduated from college with honors. One of my brothers became a corporate lawyer and enjoys playing the banjo.

Two other brothers are inventors, one in the computer industry and one in the engineering field. I once overheard a conversation in which they were discussing their individual creative processes. I gathered from their conversation that they, too, have found ways to shift from left-brain to right-brain processing.

One said that he feeds a creative notion that's percolating in his mind by reading exhaustively on the subject. He somehow knows when it's time to let go of his intellectual explorations and wait for the necessary inspiration to come to him. He acknowledged this stage of inventing as *making room for his intuition to kick in.*

The inspiration, (or what I would term the intuitive 'hit') usually arrives, he said, when he's in the shower. My other brother laughed and said the same holds true for him, and that he often bruises his head from knocking it on the shower head at that 'ah-hah' moment.

chapter two

Intuition

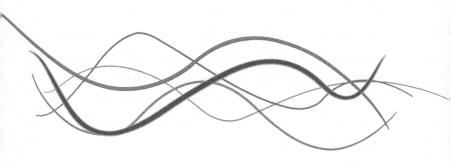

*The intuition is a growth,
primarily, in sensitivity and in
an inner response to the soul.*

**—ALICE BAILEY,
Discipleship in the New Age**

*T*rust your internal sensing. When you use it—consciously and conscientiously—it will effectively override your doubts and move you into a peaceful, receptive state of being. In this quality of being, you will open to a new sensation—a connectivity to all of life. As you tap in, infinite knowledge becomes available to you. Ask your big questions. Your answers are here.

Put in your order, a request for new information: "Is this relationship right for me?" "Is this job situation right for me?" "Which way do I go?" Formulate your question from the perspective of your Higherself. Request an answer that serves you *and others* in the best way. Maybe you don't know what your question is. Use your internal compass. What are you curious about? What gives you butterflies? Or, ask the question I ask: "What do I need to know?"

Release your expectations. (Expectation is the Ego-self trying to nail everything down.) Trust that the answers will come. Stay open and be patient.

They may come to you like a jolt of electricity. You may experience a sudden and surprising shift or a quiet epiphany. Take note of subtle turns in your life which may deliver you into new territory, and you're wondering *how did that happen?*

As you learn to trust this connectivity and the content coming through it, you'll also refine your own gifts. (The more you trust it, the more you'll get!) You'll start to recognize the very unique way in which you receive intuitive data. Maybe you are one who receives images (clairvoyant), or feelings (clairsentient). Maybe you're one who hears information (clairaudient) or receives a clear knowing (claircognizant). Through the years, I've worked with people who exhibit all of these gifts, and many who demonstrate a fascinating combination thereof.

What facilitates intuition? Softening around beliefs, switching into Observer Mode and operating from the right-brain realm of feeling and sensing open you to your full intuitive potential. Practice taking a moment to let a difficult situation breathe before allowing a reactive, triggered response to take over and pull you out of the flow. We also need to practice being present and learning to quiet the mind. It takes a deliberate, conscious intention to resist the distractions that inhibit intuition.

Switch into Observer Mode the next time you're surfing online aimlessly, after you've caught up on emails, Facebook messages and are beginning to passively absorb whatever text, images and messaging that your clicking leads to. What do you notice about your energy? Your posture? Your overall feeling?

Advertisers love this kind of passive surfing. They know all they need is a compelling story, evocative images, and directed messaging to make you believe in, and buy, whatever idea they're selling. When you find yourself following threads which encourage 'us vs. them' thinking or fosters a feeling of lack, take note of the polarizing effect beginning to work as a divider, separating you from an understanding that we're all in this together.

Make a conscious effort to resist distractions that take you out of the flow of Streaming Consciousness and cause you to miss subtle signals from your personal environment. Whenever you realize that you've gone somewhere else in your thoughts, or have been pulled far from where you were focused, take a moment to breathe back into the present moment. Look around you. Bring your attention back to the task at hand, or to what (or whomever) you were attending. It's really a matter of coming back into full and present consciousness, isn't it?

There are times when we all find it difficult to come back to the moment for whatever reason. Don't torture yourself. Another way to arrive at intuition is by taking the pathway of imagination.

Imagination

*Imagination is everything. It is the
preview of life's coming attractions.*

—ALBERT EINSTEIN

We come into this world with an unlimited capacity to learn, grow and imagine. Our intuition is very accessible when we are young because our imagination is full and active. Sadly, imagination is often an inevitable casualty of the natural process of growing up. This is the journey for most of us in becoming adults. We strive to achieve and become productive in the world, trusting our intellect and leaving 'childish things' behind. However, some of the world's most creative grown-ups are those who've held onto their child-self's wild and wonderful imagination. Brilliant artists and inventors such as Pablo Picasso and Albert Einstein have been called eccentric for their childlike inclination for play.

It's essential that you get to know your child-self in order to gain access to intuitive data that flows through Streaming Consciousness. Try to remember certain sensations in your childhood. Smell the fresh-cut grass where you played outside, hear the creaking of the swing set in the schoolyard, or see the colors in your crayon box. Invite these sensations and memories to return to you.

If you find it difficult to remember the past, call upon the Universe to assist you—"Take me to my child-self!" Release your expectations about how this might unfold. Disengage from the Ego-self. Keep your heart open and your intention clear, and reaffirm that you *will* receive memories or recall touchstone moments from the past within the next few days. Stay open to the little responses coming to you in the Stream.

Within a short time, you may see something reminiscent of favorite things from your childhood. You might unexpectedly catch the scent of cologne that reminds you of someone you loved long ago. The smell of *Jungle Gardenia* still takes me right back to my fourth grade teacher, Mrs. Ellis, and with one whiff of Old Spice, I'm back on my Gramps' front porch, jabbing my finger through smoke rings from his cigar. Memories may also flood back to you through your dream world when you program the unconscious with this sort of request.

In whatever way the Universe responds to your request, when a memory is triggered, immerse yourself in all the sensations surrounding it. Be there, beyond time, and see what else comes to you. You're likely to experience the awakening of your imaginative child-self!

Many people I've met through the years have survived difficult, often abusive childhoods by detaching from feelings too painful to feel. This coping mechanism can leave them closed off from all feelings, even good ones, and dissociated from emotions. This often leads to a total disconnect from the past in general. Many even say that their childhood is 'a blank.'

Attempts to access childhood memories can leave these people disoriented. Their emotional disconnect prevents them from experiencing deeper emotion in their adult relationships, or even with their own children. Numbed for so long, they might also experience ambivalence about many things in their present lives.

One client said to me, "When you say 'feelings,' it makes me feel confused." She also had difficulty making decisions. One must know what one feels about one thing, to decide between it and something else. Unfortunately, when feelings from the past are buried, the child-self goes underground—*and so does imagination.*

Awakening the Child-Self

*One does not become enlightened
by imagining figures of light, but by
making the darkness conscious.*
—C. G. JUNG, *The Philosophical Tree*

When I begin my work with clients, I first orient them to my way of seeing. Many, I find, are shut down emotionally. We all have scars from our past. I never hesitate to refer clients, if need be, to certified specialists who are trained to treat more complex, psychological issues. Similarly, therapists often refer clients to me when they feel that a more intuitive approach might be helpful.

I first take a few moments to merge with the client's timeless consciousness and travel through the Stream to their past. In my experience of it, it feels as though I'm becoming One with that person, and I'm able to see through their eyes in any given segment of time. I always land in a particular scene with some energy around it, containing moments that have impacted my client's journey in some way. As I experience and relate details, together we begin the process of uncovering where the shutdown may have occurred.

Once there, I look around for details of the scene and report what I'm witnessing. I invite my clients to join me there, using guided imagery to help them along, taking extra time with those who are particularly out of touch with their history.

Jack was in his early thirties, living between his parents' homes since their divorce, several years prior. He was doing menial work at the business of a family friend, not feeling particularly inspired or excited about anything, as if unable to imagine his life unfolding any differently. I felt as though he'd lost his spark. He was out of touch with his child-self and his spirit felt, to me, less vibrant as a result. My sense was that if we could reconnect Jack to his child-self in the past, we could reignite his spirit and open him up again to new possibilities in his present and future.

"Jack," I said, "tell me about something you love."

There was a long silence. I tried another approach.

"What sort of things do you like to do?"

Another long silence.

"I don't know . . . " he said.

I asked Jack to take a deep breath with me and merged with his timeless consciousness, traveling through the Stream to his past. I found myself seeing through his eyes a pivotal moment from about third or fourth grade. I relayed the experience to him as it unfolded, describing the sights and sounds around the event.

"There's someone yelling at us,'" I said, "I'm hearing a female voice. It's really loud. It makes me want to cover my ears. She's outside . . . hanging up clothes on the line."

"My mother did that." Jack confirmed. "She was always yelling at me to do my chores. I hate it when people yell."

"Are you remembering, Jack? Can you see it, too?" I asked.

"I don't remember much, but I do remember that she yelled at me all the time, especially after my Dad left. She had to go to work to support all us kids and was tired all the time. She never let me play."

I asked Jack to take another deep breath with me. My intention was to engage his imagination, access a pleasant memory from his past and create a safe haven where he might reunite with his child-self. It's often when I relate a subtle sensory experience from a client's past that a memory is triggered. Details come flooding back to them.

I instantly found myself in another moment, this time sensing it more than seeing it.

"Jack," I said, "we're tasting something cold . . . like ice cream . . . vanilla. . . ."

"Root beer floats!" Jack exclaimed. "I used to love root beer floats!" It was the first time Jack had expressed any real enthusiasm. I thought to myself, "We're in!"

I encouraged him to stay with that sensation, the taste of a root beer float, and to describe it to me.

"Velvety. Sweet. Creamy!" Jack said.

I asked Jack where his little boy-self would be enjoying that special treat.

"At the kitchen table," he replied.

"I'm there too, Jack!" I saw a red-and-white checkered oilcloth covering the table. There were others around us.

"Who else is here, Jack?" I asked.

"Everyone but my sister. She's still at school. My mother's doing dishes at the kitchen sink."

I often ask child-selves to take me to their room. It's usually a safe, protected space. Children love to show off their stuff; it's their way of saying, 'Let me show you who I am.'

I asked Jack to feel himself taking his dish to the sink, and then announcing to everyone that Louise-from-the-future is here to visit him and he's going to show her his room. "Okay," he said, "they want to come too!"

"Tell them that Louise is here for Jack . . . because he's *special!*"

"Okay," he said, "I just did. They're jealous!" Jack chuckled.

Jack stayed with me, seeing his child-self escorting me to his room. We stopped at the doorway, looking in at a set of bunk beds. I was drawn to a bookshelf in the corner.

"Jack," I said, "tell me about this book on the top shelf. It's about airplanes."

"Oh!" he said, sounding very animated, "I forgot about the book!" In that moment, I felt Jack's child-self reconnecting with Jack's adult-self.

"My fourth grade teacher gave it to me," he said. "It was a book with pictures of World War Two airplanes. I used to have dreams about flying fighter planes in the war." I could sense Jack's child-self emerging. Then he showed me a worn-out baseball.

He said he'd recently gone up in his mother's attic where he found his old baseball cards in a trunk.

"When I held them," he said, "I got the weirdest feeling—like electricity going through me!"

That electricity he was feeling was a sign that his child-self was trying to reach him.

Jack then climbed to the top bunk to look out the window at the night sky. I could feel that it was a special place. "I loved it up here," he said softly. "This is where I *talked to God*." I was moved, hearing (and feeling) Jack connecting so deeply to an important a memory.

Once a child-self connection is reestablished, our imagination is set free to take us beyond our intellect and open us to our unlimited intuitive gifts. To imagine is to go beyond thinking and shift into right-brain, intuitive sensings. We simply cannot get there via logical thoughts.

I encourage my clients to assume guardianship of their child-selves, to imagine taking them by the hand and escorting them into the now—where that little boy or little girl can be free to dream and play again.

"You are now in charge of your child-self," I told Jack. "It is your job to protect him and love him and have fun with him! Take his hand and bring him into his future, where you are right now."

Jack had a follow-up session a few months later. He said he felt as though he was making friends with his child-self, inviting him in more and more. Every so often he takes out the baseball cards and they go through them together, picking out their favorite players.

No Child-Selves Left Behind

For the purpose of awakening the imagination and expanding intuition, I find it impossible to leave out the child-self. Here's what you can do to help awaken your own child-self who can lead you back to your imagination and into heightened intuitive abilities:

First, ask the Universe for help. Request guidance in getting back to the child-self left behind. Drop your left-brain expectations about how you might receive this assistance. Remember, the Universe is immensely creative, with *infinite* means at its disposal. Simply affirm: *I'm excited to awaken and embrace my child-self!* Unexpected, synchronized surprises will assist in re-acquainting the two of you.

Memories may come to you, perhaps in dreams, and you'll feel as though you're really there, beyond time. In our dream world there is no time or space. Or, you might run into someone from your past that reminisces about long-forgotten memories, which may open up a whole pocket of memories. A little toy or game resembling one from your childhood might catch your eye as you pass by a store window. If you decide to purchase and take it home with you, put it in a special place!

Engage your child-self in fun ways. Make goofy mouth noises. Make faces in the mirror. Roll down a hill or (if the body's willing) do a cartwheel, somersault or headstand. Play *Red Rover, Musical Chairs* or *Mother-May-I* at your next party!

Remind your child-self how you couldn't wait to grow up—have your own apartment, drive a car, stay up late, choose what you want to eat. Show your child-self how you've accomplished those things. Take time to feel the delight in having done so.

Get in touch with your child-self's fears. Quell them with assurances that your child-self is in good hands, that it's safe to come out and play and experience everything with that childlike sense of wonder.

There's a marvelous photo on my website that I regularly send clients to view when they're trying to reconnect with their own child-selves. The photo was taken by a friend who lives in a constant state of awe and appreciation for the magic and mysteries of life. She has a vibrant imagination, and she truly *believes.*

One day she saw a fairy on a flower across the room, (yes, *a fairy*—go see for yourself!) and she remarked out loud how beautiful it was. She asked if it wouldn't mind staying put while she got her camera. The fairy did just that, (I guess fairies like compliments) and the image came out clearly and unmistakably on film.

Wonders abound when we quiet the cynical, logical mind in favor of staying open to possibility. After all, the Universe is infinite!

Connecting with Something Greater

*Faith is the daring of the soul to
go farther than it can see.*

—NEWT CLARK, Theologian

From a state of childlike wonder, we first conceived of mysteries we couldn't see and felt ourselves as part of something wonderful and amazing. We were naturally open to ponder big ideas and believe in miracles. Reconnecting with our child-selves re-engages in us a sense of awe, allowing us again to reconnect to something greater in our lives. We begin to see ourselves as a crucial part in this vast human experience, and live far beyond the small dreams of the limited, Ego-self.

Once we reorient ourselves and are able to operate from the context of these grander ideas, we begin to comprehend the lessons life gives us—some over and over again, packing serious wallops! From this vista, we can see that even painful life lessons help evolve us toward our very own special purpose in the world.

As with many people, I was awakened spiritually through devastating circumstances—the one-two punch of losing of my father when I was nineteen and my mother when I was twenty-three. The overwhelming sense of loss left me feeling desperate for answers.

I was working as a researcher and music therapist in behavior modification. While I witnessed how shaping and modifying human behavior can improve people's lives, the work didn't give me a deeper understanding of the human condition. It didn't help me address matters of the soul, such as—Who am I? Why am I here? Where am I going? These were questions coming up for me and I needed someone to help me answer them. I sought guidance from an elder of the church where I grew up. Though she couldn't help me find answers, she was comforting (and later, I would realize, quite intuitive).

"Your grief will awaken you," she said.

My father wasn't there to give me away at my wedding, and my mother died before I had my children. I was living with a growing sadness, a difficult marriage, and felt more and more like an outsider in my conservative Southern California community.

An old friend from high school in Pasadena was involved in the burgeoning Transcendental

Meditation® movement, and introduced me to the technique. With TM®, I was able to create space between the story of myself I was beginning to believe —that I would always carry a profound loneliness— and the reality that nothing exists but the present moment, that I am neither my thoughts nor my experiences, but connected to something far greater, and I am here to do my best to be a light in the marketplace.

As my meditation practice grew and changed (I went on to study many techniques and disciplines), my intuition, which had always been strong, started to evolve further. I'd often be tuning into people— mentioning things offhandedly that I couldn't have known, completely oblivious that I was doing so.

I began the study of metaphysics, which supported fascinating explorations into 'that which is beyond the physical' and seemed to have answers to many of my questions concerning life—and what we call death. I took a few intuition classes, practiced my gifts with friends, and even worked for a time at 'Magic Island,' a private club fashioned after the Magic Castle in Los Angeles. It was there that I learned how I would *not* choose to use my gifts. People often asked me embarrassing and inappropriate questions, inquiring about lovers (while spouses stood nearby).

My journey took me deeper into exploring the meaning of life—and death—and everything in between. It inevitably guided me into my life's work as an intuitive spiritual counselor. It has been enhanced most greatly by the gift with which I was born—a trust in my own connectivity to an expansive, infinite energy that is far greater than myself.

In past years, I've felt conflicted about the predominent religious interpretation of that power as patriarchal, when my experience of it is beyond any limiting classification. I began to refer to this energy as 'the Source'—my way of honoring anyone's interpretation or belief in a higher power, or lack thereof. This is important, as I have clients from all religious backgrounds and even some from the atheist camp.

I've come to realize that experiencing a connection to something greater isn't exclusive to any one belief system. An atheist client has experienced this connection, referring to it as 'presence' (note lowercase P)—as in being in the present moment with everything else. As for me, I've always had an unmistakable sensing that this unconditionally loving presence is God.

We also have an elevated, overseeing aspect of our consciousness that operates in alignment with God, in stark contrast to our smaller, Ego-self. I call this the Higher-self. The ego gives us a temporal identity, a character to play on the earthly stage. When we access the Higher-self, we're lifted to greater vision and purpose, overriding the limited perceptions of the Ego-self, driven by fear or a sense of lack—of love, power, control, or material things.

However you perceive it, a belief in something greater gives you hope and comfort, but even more, it opens your mind to receive new knowledge, healing, and even miracles.

Trusting my own connectivity to God has allowed what I call *the voice* to reach me on occasion. I receive clear and unmistakable words, and trust the source of these words—the messages are always useful, loving, and for the greater good of all!

I first heard *the voice* several years ago, toward the end of an in-person consultation.

"Louise, now it's time for you to show people moments when they've known God!"

Yipes, I thought, this is new!

"Okay, sure," I replied in my thoughts, "I'm game!"

Since that moment, I'm often interrupted in consultations by what appears to me as a flash of light and an image which opens up onto a larger screen. I'm shown an instance, one in which my client *has known God.* These flashes usually correlate to profound moments of feeling *alive, connected,* or *at peace.*

The very first time I experienced this, I said to the client,

"I see a lake. It looks as though you're fishing, around the time you were in fourth grade. You're not alone. There's someone who feels like an elder family member, a male."

My client remembered the precise moment it occurred, one summer while fishing on a lake with his Uncle Joe. He said that he'd never forgotten the feeling that came over him—the feel of the air, the color of the sky, the sound of the fish jumping in the water, the smell of the trees at dawn. He said he had a deep and utter knowing, that "all's right with the world!" This, to me, is what knowing God feels like.

These amazing moments in our lives serve to introduce us, and bring us, to a certain frequency of connectivity. We sense our connection to the Divine, beyond this physical experience. The Buddhists call it Zen. The Hindus: Nirvana. The sports world refers to it as 'being in the zone.' (And at least one atheist calls it presence.)

The greatest value in sharing these bright spots with my clients is the validation they receive of their own personal experience of connectivity to something far greater. Most often, they simply had not defined those moments as such. Within the last five years or so, I'm finding people beginning to recognize their own connectivity to a greater force in humble and beautiful ways. Through spiritual practices, learning from enlightened teachers and inspirational books, and experiencing déjà vu and countless synchronicities, millions of people are being empowered with this truth: their connection to that force is within them and is experienced by them as a feeling in their body and being, in moments simple and profound.

If you are unable to relate to these experiences yet, don't fret. Stay open. Be present. Allow and welcome what the world brings to you. If at some point, you feel a need to react in some way, wait it out. Pause for a second, switch into Observer Mode, and come back into the present moment. Look around you, and take it all in. You may see things differently, receive a sudden insight, or feel your heart open to let someone in!

The Way In—Sensory Mechanisms

Visual imagery (the ability to consciously picture something in the imagination), is a powerful mechanism that facilitates intuition. There have been numerous scientific studies exploring its effect on the brain. Results show that visualized images register in the brain as distinctly as images processed in through visual cortex. In other words, the brain records imagined movement or activity as if having been physically experienced in the body.

However, not everyone thinks in images. I felt one apprentice's energy retract when I said the word 'visualize.' She disclosed that the process of visualizing had always been a chore for her, and said she was exclusively clairaudient. I asked a few questions to confirm her sense orientation, tried again with the word 'imagine,' and we were right back on track.

When I merged with her timeless consciousness in the Stream, I heard chickens clucking and cows mooing. She confirmed this was at her aunt's farm, where she'd loved spending time as a child. She described her aunt as a free spirit.

"We're standing near a fence," I said, "looking into a corral of horses. There's something going on—an understanding without words."

"Yes," she said, "My aunt and I used to call horses to the barn with our minds."

Childhood memories came flooding in. She said the farm was the only place she ever felt free to be herself, and until now, she'd never felt comfortable trusting that she could communicate in this way.

As part of the evolutionary shift in consciousness, more and more people are becoming sensitive to subtle energies and even feeling what others feel. These empaths must take special care to learn how to draw boundaries around themselves and not absorb others' stuff as their own. I often work with empaths to help them create their own decoding system to distinguish physical sensations they tend to pick up from others, particularly when they're most susceptible—out in public, and specifically in large crowds.

Scott is an apprentice who commutes every day by train to his job as a business consultant. Because he is so extremely empathic, he'd been wrestling with an increasing resistance to his daily travel. He related that the moment he stepped into a passenger car, he'd be overcome with feelings of extreme worry and panic, and for a time thought that he might have an anxiety disorder. In touch with his intuition, he also worried that these fears signaled some sort of premonition about a future disaster or train accident. We explored these experiences further and came to find that, in fact, he was simply being bombarded by worries and concerns emanating from other passengers.

I suggested to Scott that each day, as he stepped into the car, he tap the outside of the train, visualizing a line of protection drawn between his and others' emotions. (This is something I always recommend for sensitive people to do when in a crowded place.) The sense of containment and safety within his own boundaries would fill him with a sense of incredible peace and wellbeing.

This tool became immediately useful and wonderfully effective for Scott. He reports that with each tap, he now feels a discernable change in his own energy. It addition, he can feel the vibrations of other passengers becoming entrained onto his higher, more expanded, loving—and fearless—frequency! He senses a sudden calm move throughout the train.

Try these simple exercises to flex your intuitive muscles:

Whenever you start to look at the clock or your watch—just know the time! (Access it from the Stream!) Then check the results.

Tell yourself the weight you're about to see registered on your scales before you step on.

Let the name of the person calling you come before you pick up the phone or check your Caller ID!

Many people visualize their parking space before they get there. Take it a step further and pull (from the Stream) the color of the car you'll find next to yours, once you've parked in your designated spot!

And a few reminders:

Guide yourself back to the present moment. Resolve to make an effort to resist distractions. Become the observer of your thoughts—and remember to pull out of those thought loops. Work to awaken your child-self, and revive your imagination by being playful. Embrace a belief in an energy, power or presence greater than yourself. Start to trust your own unique way of sensing and you'll find yourself flowing in the Stream!

chapter three

Functionality

*How wonderful it is that nobody
need wait a single moment before
starting to improve the world.*

—**ANNE FRANK,**
Diary of a Young Girl

*E*mbracing a life of authenticity, love and community deepens our connection to life and puts us in the flow of Streaming Consciousness. We gain access to a magnetic force—a Current of Unity—when we reach out to others in ways that are non-judgmental and not ego-driven. When we repeat old, unconscious patterns, we are pulled out of this unifying Current and miss chances to interact spontaneously, receive (and contribute) fresh new ideas—and to connect. I describe the particular feeling of Oneness as the deep heart connection I feel when watching people pull together after a crisis or tragedy. All for one—and one for all!

Everyone has tough times. This is how life works. The key is to greet challenge with curiosity and not let it spin us into self-pity. Switch into Observer Mode. When we observe ourselves, we can see our own patterns coming up and pulling us into fear or martyrdom. How do we pull out of these stagnating feelings and back into our expanded selves?

One way, as my Gramps used to tell me when I felt sad or grumpy, "Go do three things for others." This kind of gesture takes us out of our own thought loops, and extends us beyond ourselves when we become self-absorbed or stuck in the lower frequency of the Ego-self.

Everyone has the power to have an uplifting effect on another. When we're feeling positive, having faith, and reframing our challenges in ways that make us feel hopeful and inspired, we are in the flow of Streaming Consciousness. When we're in that flow, we entrain others who join us in experiencing greater togetherness. I've received this gift of entrainment in some unexpected places.

I was in New York City, putting together notes for a presentation I was due to give in London, feeling very tired and uninspired. I observed my own patterns rising up—self-judgment and insecurities stemming from my relentless, perfectionist tendencies. I was beginning to convince myself that I'd never be ready in time.

I decided to take a break and venture out to get a bite to eat at a favorite spot near Lincoln Center. I'd just missed a train as I entered the subway station, so I sat down on a bench to wait for the next one. A young gal, probably in her 30s, sat down next to me. She was very thin and her clothes were threadbare.

I felt an impulse to judge her appearance and switched immediately into Observer Mode. I took a deep breath and allowed myself to open my heart to compassion and, in my mind, surrounded her in light. The gal turned to me and grinned from ear to ear. She was missing a few teeth, but her sweet smile was warm and genuine. I smiled back.

"I'm on my way to a D.A.A. meeting. That's Drug Addicts Anonymous," she said. "I'm on my twenty-third day clean."

This gal obviously was facing many challenges, far more than I might have imagined just looking at her.

"You know, I keep reminding myself that I could be just five minutes from a miracle!" she said. "That keeps me going!"

I could feel her energy absolutely lift mine. She had entrained me, elevated me onto her frequency of positivity and optimism.

"You're so right," I said to her. "Thank you for the reminder!"

I went on to have a nice dinner and then returned to finish my work, which was quick and easy. The way this stranger had reached out to me was exactly what I'd needed. Had I indulged my initial reaction and turned away from her, I would never have received the gift she brought. Inspiration often comes from places you'd least expect. In those moments, we become One.

The magnetic force of the Current of Unity also pulls in those I interpret for in consultations, friends and family of clients afflicted with symptoms of Alzheimer's, dementia, coma and stroke. I merge with their timeless consciousness in the Stream. They transmit easily and are very engaged with all that is happening beyond their physical functioning.

I first felt this when a mutual friend of a well-loved yoga teacher inquired about her in a consultation, our friend having been diagnosed with Alzheimer's. Her husband cared for her for several years with loving patience, before finally placing her in a special-care residence. I had received the occasional report, that she was happy and well, participating in her care and daily tasks.

The *moment* my client inquired about her, there she was, not only showing herself in the Stream— for the three of us had always been in sync, *in the flow*—but also our ongoing and eternal love for each other pulled us, for a brief moment, into the Current of Unity. The feeling was so tremendous, it brought tears to my eyes. We were One.

"I'm fine!" said our old friend, transmitting as if fully present, lucid and focused. To me it felt as though she was on sabbatical, still hanging out in physical form, but having a respite from the years of managing her life's challenges.

"It's the first time no one's asked anything of me!" she said.

She proceeded to project details regarding memories and events that she and my client had shared. She was not suffering. Her timeless self was exploring another facet in the physical body.

Those moments in the Current remind us how truly connected we are. The next time you feel yourself pulled into the Current, allow yourself to become fully immersed in it, and see if you can sustain the feeling of Oneness for just a little while longer. Let the moment fill you up. Hold it and expand with it. You'll be extending the Oneness of the planet, which is a powerful thing to do.

Our ability to connect with the timeless energy of souls existing in *or* out of the body is truly a gift we've been given in this lifespace. At the same time, a gift we give to others, equally as important, is learning to let go when the time is right. Many souls ready to transition back into the non-physical extend their stay here out of obligation to us. Our own fear tells us there are things undone, unsaid, or unresolved. We may demand or beg that they fight their way back.

Life is messy. Often there are things that never get resolved. Still, we must hush the Ego-self and surrender ourselves to the truth that we all must face this transition one day. It's unfair to try and hold others here when moving on will release them from the limitations of the body, from suffering, from struggle. Give your loved ones the blessing to go on, when they are ready, to the next higher level of their journey. Simply feel them in your heart and send forth the thoughts, *You're now free to experience the fullness of who you are! You are forever surrounded by the love of all who know you.*

The grieving process is important. Allowing ourselves to feel the pain of loss deepens us as evolving souls. It also enriches our experience here as physical beings, opening us to feel the greater heights of joy as well. Most of all, experiencing the death of a loved one brings us back to the moment, reminding us that THIS is where our true power is. We're here to feel it all. When emotion is given expression and validation, it can then move, heal, and transform our lives.

As you keep working to soften your beliefs and perceptions, to re-acquaint yourself with your child-self and imagination, and as you practice switching into Observer Mode, a subtle but distinct shift occurs. Your vibration raises and opens you to life-changing insights. From this expanded perspective, gifts will flow to you in Streaming Consciousness. Your perceptions about time will change. Yours will be a more vital and vibrant connection to life and to others, attracting greater happiness and well-being. You'll find your life expanding in all directions, elevating and empowering you. You will be positioned to attract, and manifest, infinite possibilities.

Flowing Beyond Time

But time remains an abstraction, a riddle that exists only in our minds.

— GERNOT WINKLER, director of time services at the U.S. Naval Observatory

We're obsessed with time. As soon as we learn to count we're taught to *tell* time, to be mindful of how we *spend* our time—to be careful not to *run* out of time—and that we should always *arrive* on time. Our entire physical experience is oriented around, and gauged by, time. Dr. Larry Dossey in *Recovering the soul: A Scientific and Spiritual Search* writes: "Adherence to locality in time—always looking ahead or behind, never dwelling in the moment long—has become a morbid obsession." It's difficult to separate ourselves from the idea of time being a constant.

But, it fact, all of time swirls around you in the present moment. You'll sense this with greater certainty the more you experiment with the functionality of the Stream. Being quiet and still in the present moment is the way to experience timelessness. We touch in on this in meditation. We also experience timelessness in our dream world.

Our timeless, unbounded energy flows ahead of our physical self. One could even say that we often arrive at our destination before we get there! This is my explanation for the phenomenon known as déjà vu—the physical self is catching up with the energetic, etheric self that's gone on ahead. We feel as though we've been there before—because we have!

If you've experienced unfolding synchronicities in your life, you have a sense of the cosmic-like orchestration that can occur beyond time, getting you to just the right place at just the right moment. You receive an answer to something before you've formulated the question. You meet the new tenant, employer, or car-buyer before you've even placed or answered the ad. Once accustomed to the being in the flow of Streaming Consciousness, you'll experience many more adventures that take you outside the boundaries of linear time.

The No-Time Zone

Loved ones in the non-physical dimension exist in a 'no-time zone.' When we drop the body we gain access to all of time, as we do in the physical when we participate consciously in the Stream. In the course of my work, I've come to realize that we're moving into a different kind of reality that closely resembles the non-physical experience, one that is not anchored in the constraints of time.

I sample the non-physical reality of loved ones in consultations by merging with their timeless consciousness in the Stream. I'm able to experience through them how hearts connect beyond time. Together, we relive a loving moment from years before when they were still in physical form. We might also go to a scene occurring since their passing to confirm specific moments of connectivity when those still in the physical felt them in their hearts or met with them in their dreams.

I view sneak peeks of future 'cosmic winks' these souls promise to send my clients. I see through their (etheric) eyes an expanded view of their lives, a version that overrides the fears, judgments and prejudices engrained in them while still in the body.

I've also sampled a delightful assortment of personal 'heavens' experienced in the non-physical. I meet with souls on idyllic golf courses, in sunny meadows and in lush, colorful gardens. I join them at poker games with their long lost pals or fellow service members. I share in their last physical sensations, hearing whispered words of love and support, smelling the scent of perfume or flowers in the room, and then I feel the effervescence and sense of freedom they experienced at the moment of their release.

I believe that this blending of physical and non-physical awareness through Streaming Consciousness is an experience that will be shared by all who are awakening and aware—those who remain open. A new understanding about consciousness itself will have us manifesting faster, comprehending multidimensional concepts and utilizing our extrasensory abilities.

Whenever I take clients, apprentices and audiences with me on excursions into the no-time zone, I ease them gently into the notion that moving forwards and backwards in time through the flow of Streaming Consciousness is really *no big deal*. Though I'm encountering an increasing number of those who are truly able to stay with me, wherever the journey takes us, it's still a big leap for some.

In a Monday apprentice session, I introduced Roberta to 'Future Fridays'—a fun exercise that enables us to retieve small details from the future. I sometimes suggest to apprentices that they visualize, imagine, or feel themselves floating gently in the Stream on a raft which floats upstream (to the past) or downstream (to the future). I also might suggest they find a secret passageway with stairs leading them up to a future moment, or down to a moment existing in the past. I might usher them into an imagined time capsule, which moves backward and forward in time through Streaming Consciousness.

Once Roberta and I were in sync, I used the time capsule imagery to take her with me to the upcoming Friday afternoon. I felt us landing in her home office. I described a few things that I saw around the room— her desk, a potted plant, a framed picture and a few other objects.

"Everyone has those things in their office," she said, (her left-brain interjecting its typical, rational interpretation of things). I deliberately zoomed in on the framed picture and described my impressions of three people in the photo. I felt her skepticism soften and her energy shift from left to right brain. Then I felt her (non-physical) presence beside me in that future moment.

"I get the feeling that in this particular moment on Friday," I said, "that you're needing to remember to put something outside, out in front . . . for the mailman? . . . or for trash pickup?"

"Friday is my recycling day," she replied.

"Okay," I said. "Don't forget!"

By the end of our session, Roberta was excited about having traveled to the future. And then, once again, I observed her left brain intervene:

"But how do I know that we *really* went there?" she asked.

"How would I have known that Friday is your recycling day?" I replied.

Friday night I got a voicemail from Roberta.

"Hi, Louise, it's me," she said. "Guess what I forgot to do?"

Fish Hook Technique

Here's some imagery that might help to shift your perceptions about time. It's a technique that not only demonstrates our multidimensional capabilities, but also serves as an example of its functionality:

Let's say you've got a big event coming up. You're in charge of organizing the whole deal. You're thinking there's no way you can get it all done in time! You're losing sleep. You're beginning to convince yourself that you're going to fail. It's not going to work. People will be disappointed. You can feel the stress in your body whenever you think about it. You know you're making a mountain out of a molehill, but you're finding yourself more and more worried and stressed. You're procrastinating to no end. You're barking at people for no reason. YOU NEED HELP!

Imagine that you're going fishing in the Stream. You have a boat. You put your boat in the water, and you point it downStream. Once you're in this Stream, quiet and centered, you can direct your thoughts backwards or forward in time—to the past, or to the future. In Streaming Consciousness the current moves in both directions.

Be there ... opening up your senses to all that's around you ... cool breeze.... hearing the sound of birds overhead, the slow swish as the boat moves along in the Stream ... really feel it!

Then do a mental scan—itemizing in your mind all the things that have to get done—arranging for food and entertainment ... invitations ... getting your outfit to the cleaners ...

Next, imagine that you're tossing out your fishing line—a magical fishing line that goes beyond time! You're tossing your line downStream—to that future event! Attached to your hook are all those things on your mental list that must get done.

You feel a tug. You've caught it! You're now connected to that event! Feel yourself there, halfway through your wildly successful evening.

Hear the upbeat chatter of the happy guests ... smell the food, being served ... feel the sleeve of your freshly pressed clothing against your skin ... your sense of relief—and gratitude—about how beautifully and effortlessly it has all come together! BE THERE! You can laugh, go ahead. You amaze even yourself!

Now imagine yourself taking the boat back to the shore. Tie it up good. You'll want to go fishing again. And by the way, the fishing rod has this unique quality. You can fold it up tiny and *put it in your hip pocket. The line, too, by the way, is magical. It's still connected to that future moment. But it's tangle-resistant. Wherever you go, it's with you, slowing drawing you toward that future moment.*

All through the coming days, be present, show up and attend to all that you need to do. The moment you start to worry or stress, return briefly to that future moment. Feed it, with that feeling of relief— mission accomplished! You can even pull out the rod and crank the reel a few times to reconnect yourself with that future moment.

You'll sleep better. Things will come together. You'll even get excited about it. Notice the way the event draws you toward it—closer and closer. You always knew you could do it!

chapter four

Diving Deep

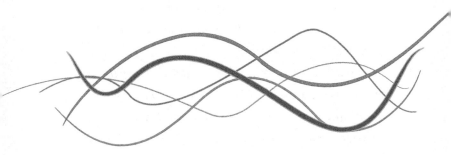

*Nearly everything is really interesting
if you go into it deeply enough.*

**—Richard P. Feynman,
American Physicist**

*D*uring our physical experience on the earth plane, most of us believe we're limited to the exclusive use of verbal and written words—collected, assembled and collated into some orderly, linear sequence—to convey what we want to express. Some of us, however, came in knowing there is far more to this physical experience than we can see, touch, hear, smell, and taste. Others learn along the way. You may be new to these ideas. Just suspend your disbelief for a bit. See what happens.

Multidimensionality is the word I use to convey the complexity of the information available in the flow of Streaming Consciousness. It's vast, multi-layered, nuanced in meaning and purpose, and timeless in its relevancy. It contains embedded themes and messages, as well as symbols and far-reaching concepts. As we continue to evolve, to understand these concepts, we'll also arrive at new and innovative ways of decoding, deciphering, and utilizing this rich and enlightening information.

As we ease into an understanding of multidimensionality, we must remain open to new ways of receiving, transmitting and interpreting information by methods that extend beyond language as we know it. Opening our understanding in this way will point us toward eventual communication with higher forms of intelligence as, increasingly, evidence will reveal that we are not alone in the Universe.

Many people have already jumped in with both feet, and have begun to notice their own multidimensional impressions. Some are ready to explore deeply, the ways in which they might participate in this type of expansion in consciousness. They're ready to dive deep!

Grounding the Wire

Right-brain sensing brings you into the flow. A feeling of wonder and optimism positions you to experience a new way of receiving. Even a mild curiosity about knowledge existing beyond old beliefs and perceptions can open you to vastly different experiences from anything you've ever known. It's always important, however, to be discerning.

Develop good judgment about new information that comes your way. Take a step back and remain in Observer Mode. Your own filter evolves over time, and it becomes easier to discern what holds truth and value by what resonates for you.

Some spiritual seekers initially find it difficult to resist the lure of far-out modalities and all the accompanying (and sometimes expensive) accessories that can divert them from the hard work involved in traveling the spiritual path. If it is your intention to grow and evolve spiritually, then new ideas must bring you answers that expand and enhance your life, and not keep you dependent on devices or others' guidance.

It's exciting stuff, but when we feel the impulse to convince or indoctrinate others, it's often an indicator that our Ego-self is taking control. Folks can take things too seriously on their spiritual path. Some even forget to laugh at themselves. Finding humor lifts the spirit and opens the heart. Enlightenment occurs in those lighter moments.

While it's true that gifts accessed through Streaming Consciousness can take you far beyond the bounds of the physical body and into abstract concepts, the real work is in integrating your abilities into practical, everyday life solutions. Successfully managing finances, participating fully in relationships, and thriving beyond loss are ways that most of us are challenged to stretch beyond our (perceived) limitations. We must rise to these challenges and continue to strive to become more responsible, innovative, patient and loving in our daily lives. Our everyday experiences serve to 'ground the wire' in our physical existence, forcing us to get real and stay present.

Receiving multidimensional information is akin to multitasking. New, rich, layered meanings may come from several directions at once or in rapid succession. A person you'd never expect to be 'into this sort of thing' might deliver a message unknowingly. (If you try to explain to them the part they play, they may think you're off your rocker.) You may uncover layers of meaning in things. I'm always exploring effective and innovative ways clients may work with this kind of information, while also continuing to ground the wire!

I encounter many people who are overdue in receiving validation for their unique intuitive gifts and multidimensional ways of perceiving. They've felt alone and isolated, judged by their families and communities, but will soon come to experience greater acceptance and togetherness in the Current of Unity. It's only a matter of time.

Telepathy

Once you've begun to touch in on Oneness in the Current of Unity, it's only a short hop into an understanding of telepathy, simply by the nature of all living organisms being energetically connected, organically and quite naturally in physical *and* non-physical dimensions.

Telepathy is a specific type of communication that involves the transmission of information from one person to another without using any of the five sensory channels or physical interaction. You participate in this phenomenon all the time. However, unless you're open, accepting and attuned to it—you might never know.

You're experiencing telepathy when you think to call your best friend, the phone rings, and when you pick it up, it's him. Or when you say certain words that come to you out of the blue, and the person you're talking to says the exact same words. You're picking up on their thoughts, and/or they're picking up on yours, all of the information flowing freely between the two of you in Streaming Consciousness.

Telepathy doesn't work like smelling, hearing, tasting, touching or seeing. When I experience telepathy, the information comes through swiftly and clearly—in a flash. It's a sort of 'knowing,' almost like a thought that isn't my own. But not just a regular thought. It's more of a super-thought, imbued with input from all the senses.

A client once asked me if I'd be able to interpret for her non-physical grandmother, born and raised in Greece, who didn't know a word of English.

I explained that telepathy is not language-specific, and does not rely on verbal communication. For me, it feels as though a mere dot of information arrives, infused with meaning that extends beyond a hundred words. A loved one might project a characteristic or pantomime a culturally specific gesture, but no words are ever necessary.

Babies transmit to me all the time through Streaming Consciousness. I attribute their ability to transmit so easily and clearly to their ongoing state of consciousness, living exclusively in the present moment. Infants before a certain age have yet to 'individuate,' or perceive themselves as *separate* from their external world. Experiencing themselves as part of everything and everyone, they hold no perception of separation from anything 'out there' and have no real fears, except for those at a very instinctual level. Their physical experience is, for a while, also unrelated to linear time. Therefore, there exists for them neither a past to regret, nor an unknown future to fear. There is only the present moment.

I was presenting on a metaphysical-themed cruise years ago, when I happened to pass a young family in a stairwell onboard the ship. My eyes briefly caught those of a tiny baby girl, nestled comfortably in the arms of her adoring mother. I stopped to coo with the baby for a quick moment, exchanged smiles with the proud parents, and then continued making my way up the stairs. Suddenly, I received a direct telepathic transmission from the baby—

"I WANT A PUPPY!"

When I received the transmission, I paused for a moment, as I always do when I receive a message. I either get an urge to share it, or the information passes quietly. In this case, I felt nudged to deliver the message. I called after to them to wait a moment. Luckily, due to the nature of the themed cruise, I didn't have to give them a context within which they could better understand what I was about to tell them.

"This little one just told me she wants a puppy," I said.

"Hey, that's funny!" the father said. "We were just discussing possibly getting a dog!"

"Where do you think you got the idea?!" I asked, pointing to the baby. She looked up at me and smiled, and we all had a good laugh.

Once you realize that everything (and everyone) in life is a vital, pulsating energy, connected in Streaming Consciousness, it's easy to entertain the possibility that we can communicate with all of creation in a fun and fulfilling way. Just trust in your innate ability to interact telepathically and be willing to engage your playful imagination. Most importantly, keep an open heart.

If you've ever watched an animal, perhaps your own pet, staring up above your head, one of two things is likely to be happening. They're observing your thoughts, seeing them as pictures, like dialogue bubbles in a cartoon strip, or they may be communing with non-physical pals. (It's all the same to them, seeing the energy of those in *or* out of the body!) While I can only interpret their projections from a human reference point, messages from trees, flowers and animals come through clearly.

Dogs often transmit images of leashes hanging by their master's front door, or favorites toys hidden in baskets, closets, and under beds. Dr. Rupert Sheldrake explores telepathy with animals in his book, *Dogs That Know When Their Owners Are Coming Home.* You may have noticed your cat reacting to an upcoming visit to the vet, even before you've pulled out the carrier. Their timeless selves already know what's in store for them. Service dogs can detect energetic change in people with epilspsy or the imminent passing of a patient in hospice. Animals have a keener sense about changes in energy and the natural process of transitioning from the physical to the non-physical.

I once had fun telepathizing with a squirrel. I was seated in the dentist's chair, awaiting my turn with the hygienist, looking out the window at a tall tree. A fat squirrel was scurrying back and forth high up along the two thickest branches of the tree. I decided to try and engage the squirrel in a little game of telepathy.

First, I brought myself fully into the present moment, into the Stream, by taking a nice deep breath. Then I drew my awareness into my body, feeling my limbs, torso, relaxing my shoulders, my jaw (I was at the dentist, after all). Finally, I opened my heart to the feelings of love and appreciation for all of God's beautiful creatures.

I projected those sentiments directly to the squirrel. I envisioned a telegraph wire running between the two of us, and then imagined a series of pictures depicting the squirrel coming right up to the window to greet me. As I continued to transmit, I watched the squirrel scamper up and down the tree, coming closer and closer to the office building. Finally, he disappeared for a few minutes and then jumped right up on the window ledge, looking right at me for a few long moments.

The door swung open and I watched my new friend jump down and run back the tree to the highest branch.

"Hey. I've never seen him come up to the window," said the hygienist, starting to assemble her tools.

That's because no one ever invited him.

My children and I were walking through the woods in Yosemite. After exploring for a while, we began searching for the way back to the lodge where we were staying. A fox appeared before us. *Let's all get at one with the fox,* I said, eager to demonstrate yet another metaphysical principle to my offspring. (They rolled their eyes, but continued to watch.) I opened my heart, felt the Oneness—and then I sent love.

The fox looked directly at me, and then started to leave. He looked back again, as if communicating that we should follow. And so we did. Sure enough, our foxy friend led us through the forest and out into a clearing located right next to our hotel.

Years ago, at the close of a presentation, I approached a young gal in the audience, perhaps in her thirties. Her energy felt vibrant and bright.

"There's something about you and trees!" I said.

"I *adore* them!" she said.

The gal later came for a private consultation. When I merged with her timeless consciousness in the Stream, I was interrupted by the image of a tree. Then it became animated and seemed to be moving closer.

"Um, it's . . . it's as if a tree-person is coming our way!" I announced to my client. I had absolutely no clue as to what this was all about, but the tree was persistent. It was holding out something in its branchy hand.

"It looks as if it has a gift for you," I said.

Then it was gone. We finished the consultation and went to join my hostess, who greeted us at the end of the hallway. She lifted a framed watercolor off the wall and handed it to my client.

"Here," she said to my client, "Something told me to give you this!"

It was a painting of a tree!

All of life speaks to us. Our own transmissions are received on the other end when they come from the heart. We're all together and connected in the flow of Streaming Consciousness. Try sending your pet a scene of something you'd *prefer* that he/she be doing, such as sleeping in a special bed (rather than on the couch), or eating from its own dish (rather than the other pet's). Focus on the positive behavior. Give it a try and see what happens!

Experience telepathy for yourself. Experiment with *being at one* with nature. Feel the connectivity within your entire being, and then try communing with a flower or tree—or the next infant you pass down the aisle of the supermarket. You'll likely be pleased with what you receive in return!

Templates

Years ago, a colleague suggested I start teaching people to do what I do. Sure enough, shortly thereafter, several clients approached me individually to ask if I could help them hone their intuitive skills so they might trust them more and learn to access information on demand. Many were also hoping to find ways of integrating their abilities into their daily lives, and particularly, into their life's work. The Illuminations Apprentice Program was born.

I take this work very seriously, so it's important for me to address any questions or concerns that apprentices have before they come on board. Apprentices first want to learn how I work with information received through Streaming Consciousness. I stress the importance of directing and containing the incoming flow of information, and developing a system with which to sort the content—identifying important themes and deciphering embedded images and symbols. Finally, it's crucial that all information serves a higher purpose, has a specific context that is relevant to, and useful in, one's life. Without a system to bring the multidimensional information into the real world, it's practically gibberish.

My own template continues to evolve over time. As my clients' needs change and grow, so does my routine. Every stage of my intuiting process continues to undergo gradual transformation, whether it develops into a more effective mode of retrieving the information itself, a better way to sort through it, or clearer and simpler ways to interpret and deliver it to my clients.

In the early years, I noticed that while sitting across from my clients during in-person consultations, I'd inadvertently point myself in the four different directions from which I was receiving information: the past (I'd face left), the present (straight ahead) the future (to the right), and messages from souls in the non-physical (even further right). I found this confused my clients, who would look to where I was looking and pointing, trying to see what I was seeing and often not hearing what I was saying.

Eventually, I found that conveying the information in narrative form, as if telling them a story about their lives, gave me the opportunity to personalize the consultation and suggest practical tools. It also allowed me to demonstrate how many interpretations are possible, and that this kind of information is never concrete or absolute.

The flow of information, coming in from all four directions, eventually became so abundant and multi-layered that once collected, it was difficult for me to retain it. Hence, another new template emerged, one that I still use today:

I envision the information flowing into what appears to me as three separate video streams. I relay the content of each one to the client as I view them. As I go deeper into exploring the meaning of what I'm watching, I'm able to move each video backward to get some back-story, or forward to watch possible outcomes. Each scenario tells me something different about my client's life concerning a relationship, a job or a living situation, or a unique directional question that requires some special handling or sorting out.

The second thing many apprentice candidates want to address is their concern about intuiting ominous information, such the foretelling of imminent deaths or future disasters. Many people have been troubled since childhood by visions or dreams containing this kind of foreboding, precognitive information. I remind them that it's all out there—infinite, timeless information—available in the Stream. I show them a method that allows them to reprogram their dreams at bedtime, specifying the content they prefer to receive in their sleep. The most important thing to remember is that what we receive in the flow depends upon *our personal intent and focus.*

When we as 'receivers' set forth and stand firmly in our purpose to receive *only that which is life-enhancing, life-expanding for all, and in the light*—then so it shall be. If we choose to maintain a positive focus and a pragmatic, matter-of-fact demeanor in receiving and interpreting intuited information, the content will lack a negative or dramatic flavor. (That said, drama queens need not apply!)

I also discuss the ethics and necessary intentions involved in this work. It's tempting for many, once they gain confidence in using their gifts, to want to show off and try to impress others. After one apprentice 'read' a prospective boyfriend, she never heard from him again. Another mentioned his psychic prowess to his colleagues and was subtly (but unmistakably) excluded from future social gatherings. Practicing one's intuitive skills with another should never be done without permission, and only with an expressed intention to facilitate healing, resolution, and for the purpose of receiving greater truths for everyone.

Once I'm assured a candidate's mission and goals are in alignment with mine, we enter into a partnership with the main goal of bringing their gifts to the forefront. At the start of each session, we begin with an invocation that reaffirms our higher purpose in working together. In the first sessions, we'll use my invocation, the one I always recite before entering a consultation, class, presentation or workshop:

> *I always ask that I be a clear facilitator for the most reliable and relevant information that's for your highest good to receive, and for my highest good to deliver. I surround us with the light—for energy, protection, and to attract all good things. I ask that all information be within God's sight, and according to God's plan for our greater, eternal selves.*

After a few sessions, apprentices will have customized the invocation in whatever way it resonates for them. They begin each phone session by reciting it, after which we take a breath together to get us in sync. That first deep breath is important. When done properly, both parties will feel the instantaneous, unifying effect from the Current of Unity—becoming One.

Many hospice workers and nurses working in end-of-life care are aware of breathing into the rhythm of their terminally ill patients. By merging with their timeless consciousness in this way, they're able to offer support in a way that words and even touch may fall short in the tender transition to the non-physical. Some intuitive workers even report witnessing patients meeting with their non-physical loved ones as the spirit prepares to leave the body.

Apprentices then continue their sessions by doing a scan of my consciousness. This exercise provides an opportunity for me to give immediate feedback and confirmation concerning the information they pull in from the Stream. This can range from small physical details in my environment to momentary concerns, to everyday occurrences in my life. (One apprentice described a scene from a *Desperate Housewives* episode that I'd watched the night before! She was relieved to find that it was a television show and not drama involving me directly!)

As the sessions progress, I assist apprentices in creating and customizing their own templates for receiving multidimensional information. We use imagery that relates directly to something meaningful in their lives. For example, an apprentice who consults in business imagines that he's giving a PowerPoint demonstration—visualizing information flowing from the Stream and into an assortment of slides, as if projected on a screen. The earliest slides in the series correspond to scenes in the past, the slides in the middle to scenes in the present, and the slides at the end to future scenes. He downloads and reports what he's experiencing—from beyond time—as he imagines making his presentation.

Another apprentice is an avid gardener. She imagines her intuited information flowing from the Stream into separate planting pots. Each one contains a different category of information, whether it is time-related (past, present and future) or has to do with different aspects of a person's life—job, relationship, or messages from loved ones in the non-physical. She explores the content of each collection of data, and then interprets and discusses it with whomever she's practicing. She moves the process forward to see what will blossom in the future, and backward to see what nutrients the pot needs to make it do so. When she's finished, she imagines setting the pots outside in the perfect sunny spot and cleans her gardening tools under the hose for the next time.

Going to the Future

People want to hear about their future. However, whenever I'm asked to 'tell the future' in the manner of a classic soothsayer, I feel that this gives the impression that there's one future that awaits us all, regardless of how we choose to live our lives. This is simply *not the case*. There are many possible outcomes. Nevertheless, there are clients who grow impatient with me as I discuss certain dynamics contributing to the relentless obstacles in their lives. These difficulties are nearly always related to repeating patterns from the past and the way the same patterns play out in the present. But it's sometimes difficult for people to take responsibility for the part they play (knowingly or unknowingly) in their own misery. One client interrupted me and said,

"Can't you just skip all this and tell me what the future's going to be?"

I reminded her that all time exists simultaneously, and that when I go to possible positive future moments, there are an infinite number of paths to get there. The best way to create them is to deal head-on with unresolved issues in her past, and learn to switch into Observer Mode when her buttons are being pushed. This is the best way to make new and better choices in her present.

An optimal future moment, I told her, would reflect (*and result from*) lessons learned from her past and choices made in her present. This response took her quite by surprise. It's a bit mind-blowing when we realize that we hold the power to our future, and it bears repeating. We create different future outcomes relative to how and what we're doing and thinking in each present moment.

Interpretation

When I do consultations, symbols and images often arrive out of proportion and can be interpreted several ways, depending upon what resonates for my client. Colors can represent different things—red can indicate something imminent or pressing. Yellow often speaks of new learning, something insightful, or in a more literal sense, someone with blond hair. A 'splash of blue' usually points to eye color, a blue car, or one who tends wear that color predominantly. Pink tends to represent a loving heart or a favorite color.

Flowers have an ethereal, universal and timeless quality and show up frequently in consultations. Sometimes they convey, literally, a loved one's name—Rose, Iris, Violet, or Daisy. Scents of favorite flowers also come through to identify moments shared between physical and non-physical souls, as does the smell of pipe tobacco or cigars, aftershave or perfume, damp basements or dusty curio cabinets.

A body of water can represent a pond, a lake or an ocean. A dark or foggy mist might say something about a client (or loved one's) mood or characteristic attitude, and tangled threads can indicate a state of confusion—tangled thoughts.

Someone appearing to be facing two directions at the same time represents someone indecisive or untrustworthy. The feeling of bubbles translates as someone with an effervescent disposition, while bounciness can represent a Type A personality or hyperactivity.

A bog or accumulation of debris in the Stream will prompt me to look deeper into issues that may be blocking the flow of my client's life—unfinished business involving money matters, unresolved issues with family members, or resistance to new insights being offered through current challenges.

Throughout my life, I have always felt loved, protected and watched over. Therefore, I tend to frame things within an optimistic framework, and with a fairly light-hearted demeanor. I never receive ominous, foreboding or fear-inducing information. That's probably due to the positive filter I have in place. I'm blessed in this calling and I'm always humbled by the infinite, creatively and Divinely-inspired content of information that is so readily accessible to all of us.

Remote viewing is an exercise that helps hone the process of interpreting multidimensional information. It involves a 'receiver' who seeks impressions about an unseen target, transmitted by the 'sender' through extra-sensory means. When I conduct my homespun version of these exercises, I play the role of sender by focusing on an image on my computer screen. Apprentices receive their impressions and then type them into an online chat box.

I instruct them—"Give me color, texture, shape—don't try to name or conceptualize your impressions!" But, as quickly as they intuit their impressions, they'll unintentionally insert their own projections, reflexively trying to make sense of what they're getting in (their own) real-world terms. This is a natural tendency of the left brain to take over the process and attempt to organize thought. This gets them off the intuitive track.

One apprentice interpreted the color red as blood, when it was actually the color of the house in the photo I was looking at. She realized that she'd been feeling anxious about her husband's upcoming surgery, concerned that he might need a blood transfusion.

Another apprentice went off the rails when she interpreted her impression of horizontal, parallel lines as a roll top desk. It was a photo of an exotic glass butterfly from the Amazon. The parallel veins shown in the see-through wings were clearly horizontal. Once she'd made the quick left-brain association of the lines relating to a desk, she framed everything thereafter within the context of an office. In the corner of the photo was a splash of bright, white-ish light. Before I could get her back to just relaying color, shape, texture, she'd jumped ahead to interpret this as computer paper!

Get With the Flow and Prepare to Receive!

Here's an exercise that will let you experience how it feels to receive highly intuitive data from the flow of Streaming Consciousness:

Pair up with a friend. (You can do this in person or over the phone, or using Skype or any of the other online options.) You'll each be creating a template by choosing a certain setting through which you'll be accessing information for your partner.

Guided Information Retrieval:

Invite your partner to get comfortable, and ask her/him to uncross their limbs for a more receptive posture. You do the same.

Next, ask your partner to think of a question about which they would welcome new information. You decide on a question, too. Write it down. (Keep your questions confidential.)

Invite your partner to take a deep breath with you. It's with that first breath taken in unison that entrains you both into the frequency and allows access to the flow of infinite information available in the Stream.

Now, ask your partner to close his eyes and imagine (see or feel) himself *as if* arriving in a particular setting that you've chosen: the woods, the beach, the circus ... Lead him through a guided meditation detailing the sights, sounds, smells, tastes and sensations of this setting. This will help engage all his senses.

Invite your partner to imagine that he's coming upon a structure within the setting—perhaps a cottage in the woods, a hut on the beach, or a circus tent. Now ask your partner to go inside and report to you what they experience. Take notes as he downloads his impressions.

Those who have a more left-brain orientation might report about items one would logically find in such settings: "There's a table and chair ... a beach ball ... a clown ... " Encourage him to lighten up and have fun with the exercise by engaging his child-self. "Feel your little boy-self playing along!" Or coax him a little. "Make it up! Pretend!"

Once you've recorded all of your partner's impressions, then reveal your question.

The collection of information accessed from the flow of Streaming Consciousness may astound you. It's common for people doing this exercise to unknowingly mention specific buzzwords that relate directly to your question. They might describe a scenario that targets your question, or may report detailed information in the form of an analogy that gives you more clarity. Don't forget to reverse the process so that you both can practice stretching your intuitive muscles!

'The Doors'

This exercise is great when you need to make a choice between two or more possibilities. Once you've each formulated your question, list two or three possible answers that correspond to your question, as you would do in creating options for a multiple-choice question. Again, keep the questions and answers confidential.

Here's an example:
Question: What's the best direction for me to take toward getting a better job?

1) Go back to school
2) Expand my search "outside the box"
3) There's still more to learn at my current job

Ask your partner to imagine herself standing before three doors (these of course correspond to the three answers, in order, that you've already written down).

Ask your partner to go inside each door and describe fully what she experiences. Take notes as she reports what she sees, feels, hears. After that, ask her which door she'd like to go back into.

Then review all the information, discussing various interpretations, confirming details you find poignant, interesting or on-the-nose. This is a fun way to retrieve surprisingly insightful and detailed information. The answer is not always clear, but when you finally make the choice you were asking about, stay open as to how the bits of information unfold.

Have fun creating your own, customized template, a portal through which you retrieve your data and enjoy how easily accessible your intuitive abilities are becoming—and on demand! Pay close attention to the interpretation process itself, particularly as you begin to define your own unique style. Observe the tendency we all have to insert projections of our own issues and perspectives into the mix.

You may also discover that you've been unaware of a particular filter you have in place that shades how you see things (and others) in life, which causes you to add a negative or dramatic spin on how you interpret. As you switch into Observer Mode with this filter, and allow yourself to be curious about it, you'll see it transform. We often learn about ourselves when we're working with information about others. The more you work with it, the more the content tends to grow multidimensionally!

Searching for Treasure

As you start to integrate these concepts, you might feel compelled to dive even deeper into a greater understanding of multidimensionality. In doing so, you'll gain greater familiarity with the multi-layered, complex and nuanced content available in the Stream.

You may also want to try new ways of playing with the information, perhaps developing an approach that allows you to hone in on specific areas of another's life when you practice tuning into friends—relationships, specific situations, or new directions.

chapter five

The Circle, The Square and The Triangle

*The only reality we can ever truly
know is that of our perceptions,
our own consciousness,
while that consciousness,
and thus our entire reality,
is made of nothing
but signs and symbols.*

**–ALAN MOORE,
Promethea, Vol. 5**

*A*s you move forward in the Stream, you'll find greater ease in slipping back into the flow when life's challenges pull you out. Once you've experienced the marvelous Current of Unity—the energetic flow that reminds you that we're all One— you'll begin to relish more and more moments in which you feel its magnetism. You'll find that the more you appreciate these moments, the more of them you'll attract into your life!

As you make an effort to integrate Observer Mode, you'll naturally begin to let go of beliefs that no longer serve you, allow perceptions to shift, and release tired old patterns. All the while you'll be mindful of grounding the wire to ensure your heart and motivations are in the right place— *to benefit all.*

You'll enjoy exploring ways that move you into more right-brain, intuitive thinking, and discovering

pathways that lead you to back to your child-self—
that precious one who holds the key to your playful,
creative imagination. You'll also open to your own multidimensionality and begin to fathom the far-reaching
functionality and power of these concepts. All of this
points you back to the flow of Streaming Consciousness.
As you spend more and more moments in this flow,
you'll find even more abstract concepts landing right
in front of you in the Stream.

Geometric Shapes

I watched a segment of a television program about a
young autistic boy who is a math and science prod-
igy. He has been writing complex mathematical
equations since he first learned to write. When he'd
run out of paper, he'd continue writing them on the
walls of his bedroom, and then onto all the windows.
His advanced equations seemed to be coming to him
from the ethers!

In the interview, the boy demonstrated his
uncanny ability to access and conceptualize these
equations. (According to the program, some believe
his may go beyond those formulated by Einstein.)
Each time the boy was handed a brightly colored geo-
metrically-shaped cutout, he'd responded by saying,

"Oh, that's ------!"—reciting words that sounded otherworldly.

"Where do you get this information?" the interviewer asked.

"—*from the fourth dimension!*" the boy said matter-of-factly, and then giggled.

Watching this demonstration confirmed a knowing deep inside of me—that *there exists an inherent multidimensional power and language in geometrical shapes* that transcend our physical-world experience of them. In the fourth dimension, the circle, square and triangle represent geometrical archetypes with extended functionality that we are just beginning to understand and utilize. As you can see, the veil between the third and fourth dimensions is coming down.

Some, like the boy on the program, are already onboard with a new, multi-layered mode of communication. For others, these are new and mind-blowing concepts. However, the use of geometry in the construction of sacred gathering places has been around since antiquity. This direction toward a seamless third- and fourth-dimensional blending is a natural part of our evolution as multidimensional beings. Look for repeating shapes and patterns in nature. Open up to them. We can be receptive *even* to ideas we cannot yet comprehend. Start, like we did as children, with the circle, square and triangle. Here's how we've been working with them.

The Circle of Light

The shape of the circle is powerful. It represents eternity, unity, wholeness—and closure. It has no beginning and no end. It is inclusive. In the way that the Current of Unity has an inherent magnetism, the imagery of the *circle of light* initiates a similar pull that lifts you to a higher level of consciousness. Raising your frequency engages your Higher-self through Streaming Consciousness and allows you to reach others from an elevated level of intention and purpose, connecting above the fray, the drama, and Ego-self agendas. The power of the circle of light becomes activated *only* at this level of consciousness, when you participate with a *sincere intention* of facilitating resolution for the greater good of everyone involved.

Simply imagine, pretend, or feel yourself extending your energy upward into a radiant, illuminated circle of light above your head. Let that bright energy fill you with a sense of lightness and expansiveness. Then feel yourself occupying that whole space, extending upward and into the circle of light.

Invite someone to join you in the circle—someone with whom you seek better communication, greater empathy, mutual respect. Telepathize your invitation from the circle of light by transmitting clear, focused thoughts to that person's Higher-self, residing in the spirit of Oneness and reciprocal growth. This Higher-self is accessible in *everyone,* whether that soul is residing in *or* out of a physical body. Send along the invitation by transmitting through thought:

I invite you to join me in the circle of light. My heart is open and my soul is seeking wisdom and resolution.

And then communicate your intention:

I desire that greater understanding and love exist between us.

I first experienced this kind of telepathic conversation—a way to communicate Higher-self to Higher-self—several years ago. I was early for dinner plans with a friend, and was invited to wait in the cocktail lounge. Hoisting myself up onto a stool at one end of a long, horseshoe-shaped bar, I instinctively surrounded myself with light and then I looked around.

In what are normally those first few awkward moments of strangers sitting together, I then opened my heart and in an instant, felt pulled into the Current of Unity. I became intuitively aware of the Higher-selves of everyone seated around me, elevated aspects of each soul hovering just above their heads, in a circle of light.

I telepathically reached out to everyone at the bar, sending them all clear, focused thoughts from my Higher-self—wishing them happiness, the courage to live their lives in a higher way, to make a difference on the planet, and to accomplish all that they've come here to do. I felt an instantaneous recognition among all our Higher-selves—a remembering that we are all parts of the whole, all united in this journey.

Within a few seconds and practically at the exact same moment, each and every one of them turned their physical selves to look right at me! Several smiled, and one or two actually nodded! I giggled out loud, thrilled at this multidimensional moment and, when no one giggled with me, returned to the reality in which the moment began—all of us strangers, all of us living separate lives. Luckily, my friend arrived and I quickly jumped off the stool and headed to our table.

It was from this experience that I began using the circle of light to reach the Higher-selves of others in consultations. Having opened myself to, and trust-ing the validity of that incredible event, I'd given the Universe yet another pathway to reach me, and help me reach others in my work.

An interesting example of the inclusiveness of the circle, and how it seems to extend loving energy to all, occurred at the end of a consultation, when I asked my client if she had any additional questions.

"Yes," she said, "I'm concerned about my friend. She's getting more and more negative—almost *toxic*! I really don't enjoy being around her anymore!"

I coached her in how to prepare ourselves to gain entry to the circle of light, emphasizing that healing and resolution can only occur when we first take ourselves to that Higher level of intention.

I started to invite the Higher-self of my client's friend into the circle, when I observed a cat rushing in! It was a very large, seemingly agitated—perhaps *angry* kitty with beautiful markings. I mentioned this to my client and merged with the cat's timeless consciousness in the Stream.

"This is one feisty tabby," I told my client. "She wants to nip at your friend."

"It's MANDY!" my client practically shouted. "It's my friend's cat!"

Several more cats joined the circle of light. This was a first.

"I'm seeing more cats with Mandy now," I told my client. "They all seem agitated."

"My friend has several cats," my client confirmed. "I've been concerned that they've been absorbing her negativity."

She said that Mandy, previously a sweet and gentle cat, had indeed begun to bite her owner, while the other cats avoided her or hissed at her whenever she came close to them.

Animals have been showing up increasingly in consultations to assist in resolving difficult situations (they're evolving, too), so I welcomed Mandy into the circle of light.

"Hello, Kitty! We're so happy that you've joined us. We're counting on you to find love in your owner."

"Good luck!" my client snickered. I promptly reminded her to get back up to her Higher-self!

"Mandy," I said, "it's up to you to find the love in your owner. It's there *somewhere*, in everyone! Please extend the love we're feeling here in the circle of light to her, as well. She needs your extra-special care! We're backing you up!

An hour after the session, my client sent this email:

OMG! I just got a message from my friend, saying that she is going to try a meditation class tonight! This is SO not her! Is Mandy working her magic already?

I use the circle of light whenever I decide to intentionally see only the good in another. Sometimes it's hard for me to get there, especially when someone's really pushing my buttons. When Edith Ego starts yammering away, trying to jockey for some sort of better-than position, that's a cue that I'm caught in a thought loop. *(Down, Edith. Down!)*

I invite that person's Higher-self into the circle, focusing on where goodness resides within that person's timeless soul. Those positive qualities immediately become apparent to me. Shortly thereafter, I'll encounter the person and find her responding in some positive way—addressing that loving aspect of her soul. We're both elevated to a better place. The circle of light is quite an effective way to send forth a telepathic reminder that love does, in fact, abide. Always.

The Square

The square's straight, perpendicular lines convey the feeling of stability, structure, and matters relating to home, hearth, and materialism. The shape feels grounding and solid. I often suggest the use of the square as a template for apprentices to collect and sort information flowing in from Streaming Consciousness, relating specifically to one's home, work, skills or talents.

A client reported that she was feeling 'boxed in' by her job as a graphic designer. She felt that her creative talents were being wasted, and despite her best efforts, were being ignored and unappreciated by her employer. Quite spontaneously, I saw her standing in the middle of a square—the four walls of her office. I merged with her timeless consciousness in the Stream and could feel her frustration, as well as an overwhelming, claustrophobic feeling. The ceiling felt very low, as if there was no room to rise up, no place to go from there. I could understand why she felt like getting out of there.

I saw a door appear on one side of the square, which told me there would soon be a way out. But first, we needed to improve things *inside the room*, within those four walls. I cautioned my client about running away from her current job before seeing a clear move to the next job. (She had a lot of debt and not much in savings.)

It's important in any endeavor that we not be motivated by impatience, angst or fear. When we move on too quickly from repelling situations, without making room for some sort of resolution (or new learning) in the present, we risk taking our issues and lessons with us and having to confront them again down the road! We needed to find ways to improve her work situation in the present.

I looked into the square and asked to be shown what might help my client improve her job in some way to make it more pleasant and enjoyable while things could be put in place for a move forward. What appeared to me was the image of a middle-aged woman, sitting in the corner at a desk. She seemed sad and alone. Her hairstyle looked a bit outdated.

She looked up at me and smiled hesitantly. Then I got the letter V."

"Oh, that must be Valerie," said my client. "She's in accounting. She does seem a bit lonely."

"Ah-hah!" I said, "This is one way to improve your situation at work. Reach out to Valerie! This will open your heart and expand you in wonderful and unpredictable ways!"

I moved the scene forward in time just a little and felt it was appropriate to go ahead and move toward the door. When I went through it, I found myself in yet another room. In that room, the image of another woman appeared to me, tall with dark hair. She was slurping something through a straw. The name 'Natalie' came to me. I relayed this information to my client.

"Oh, this is someone that I recently met through a friend! She told me she's addicted to diet soft drinks. We really hit it off! Should I call her?"

I encouraged my client not to obsess about 'Natalie,' reminding her that we found her in that adjacent room and that resolution within her current situation was necessary before she could go through that door. I advised her to keep her energy up, stay in alignment (out of fear and ego agendas), and to make a conscious effort to release frustration about her job.

In the meantime, I suggested that she be attentive to whatever she might still accomplish at her current job, including a possible meaningful exchange with Valerie. I told her to release her worry, as well as her limiting expectations about how things might work out. (I love the expression *expectancy without expectations!*)

My client called later to report that Natalie *of all people* had called to offer her a job in her new startup business as Creative Director. By not making the first move, she positioned herself to negotiate a good salary.

You, too, can activate the effectiveness of the square by trusting there are lessons to be learned right where you are, and that when the current situation reaches a resolution, doors will appear and open to you. Imagine yourself tossing all your questions or issues concerning home, hearth or job into a large, illuminated square. Then let it all go. Release any worry or concerns, any busy or extraneous thoughts. And then, for just a few moments, redirect your thoughts somewhere else. Think about what you'll be having for dinner that evening, or fill your heart with feelings about someone you love (pets included).

Then breathe back into the present moment. Return to your image of the square. Look to see (imagine, notice or feel) what images or symbols have filled that space, and what new information is waiting there for you.

Try playing with the additional functionality of the square in ways that will activate change! Add a few windows. Open up the blinds to let in more light, or open the windows all the way to let in the fresh air! Put pictures on your walls of those who love and believe in you, or those that remind you of all you've accomplished. See what happens when you put in a door—a side door that gives you entry to related information, or perhaps a back door that takes you behind the scenes for deeper understanding of a situation. See what (or who) shows up in your life in the days that follow!

The Triangle

The upright triangle represents the male force, energy, power or steady strength, and spiritual geographical gateways. A triangle with a point facing down represents the feminine—groundedness, receptivity, openness. The apex of a triangle connotes direction or potential movement. In the same way I move forward or backward through time with my clients in Streaming Consciousness, I get a similiar sense of motion and going beyond time when I put myself in the brilliant triangle.

A client asked about a business plan she was preparing to implement. She wondered if the one she'd devised would help her meet her goals the most effectively and expediently. I merged with her timeless consciousness in the Stream and saw us in an upright triangle, which quickly became three-dimensional. A pyramid. I saw us climbing from one level up to the next as I relayed the information I found waiting for us at each of four levels that appeared to me.

We landed on the first level quickly and easily. There I saw a large 'T'—usually translating for me as telecommunications—and sure enough, my client confirmed that she'd just built a website to promote her new business.

Moving up to the second level was also an easy climb. There I saw several file folders, neatly stacked, and a large pile of CDs alongside a large computer monitor.

"Yes," she said, laughing, "I've also redone my office space. I nearly bought out the local office supply!"

To reach the third level of the pyramid I felt as though we had to hoist ourselves up, and once there, were out of breath. Someone appeared before us on the same step—an 'M,' definitely male. He was talking fast, looking quite anxious. He felt like a distraction, and his presence was slowing down our progress.

"Oh," said my client, "That would be Michael. He's my ex-husband. He recently asked me to bring him on board."

She said she'd been considering it, but had a strong hunch that since they didn't work well together as partners in marriage, they weren't likely to do so in business. This stall in progress upward confirmed her hunch.

Others joined us on the fourth and last level, potential colleagues who might collaborate with my client in her new business and align with her own higher intentions to create win-win solutions for everyone. As we closed, she said—

"By the way, my new business is an MLM venture."

I asked her what that meant.

"Multi-Level Marketing," she said laughing. "What used to be known as a *pyramid* enterprise!"

Use the triangle when you need to feel courageous—the spiritual warrior moving forward through challenges, partnering with the Universe while receiving Divine guidance! Play with imagery that gets you excited about allowing in more movement to propel you forward in your life. Do this when things are feeing static or stale. Be the bold adventurer exploring new, uncharted territory!

As I was writing about the illuminated square, I felt as though I was cruising at the speed of light! Even as I wrote about it, I felt myself surrounded by its illumination. And then my thinking stalled. I was trying to think of the best example to use. I've collected so many stories that document remarkable outcomes reported by clients and apprentices. (Alas, I could hear my editor sighing, "one more lengthy story—*Short version, please!*")

Then I thought to envision myself in the brilliant triangle, as if momentarily blocked by an ice floe. I thought to myself, *indeed, the point would make an excellent icebreaker! Let me sit here for a few minutes and see what happens while I imagine the triangle breaking through this momentary blockage.* I decided to step away and let things breathe. I left my office to go have dinner.

When I returned to the computer, I found an email waiting for me. It was from the client who'd been eager to move on from her job. She was confirming that before she had a chance to reach out to Valerie, the co-worker had shown up with a plant to beautify her office! She also confirmed that Natalie had been in touch and the two were in discussion about working together. There was my example! My customized triangle had broken through the writer's block! One more section completed!

You might feel a new, pointed determination or focus when the triangle starts moving you in a new or better direction. Let positive outcomes appear 'round the bend!' If you feel yourself coming to an impasse, trust that you'll be shown the way. Watch for markers or symbols. You might feel your triangle pulling you sideways toward one or two attractions existing in the flow. Explore them in detail.

And then continue on with your journey in Streaming Consciousness toward the best possible you.

Epilogue

The Journey

*The feeling remains that God
is on the journey, too.*

— **Saint Teresa of Avila**

*O*ur journey in this physical dimension is only one of an infinite number of treks that our soul makes on its way to finding greater truth, wholeness, and the discovery of itself as intimately connected to God. We always have a choice in how we will experience that journey.

Some souls will come to new insights during their earthly experience and realize that while we are in fact, an eternal energy, that we are having a momentary physical experience. They will begin to experience a certain flow to life in Streaming Consciousness and feel Oneness in the Current of Unity. They'll learn to position themselves in that flow in such a way as to deliberately and consciously co-create with God.

You may find it surprising to learn that souls in the non-physical are absolutely itching to return to this dimension. "Who'd want to come back into *this* crazy world?" you might ask. Only in this third-dimensional reality can we grow, experience, and evolve as physical beings—arriving in a state of forgetfulness, to then (hopefully) awaken and attempt to remember all over again from an entirely new perspective.

We're privileged for the opportunity to participate in the expansion of consciousness that's happening at this time on the planet—and in the entire Universe. It's important to play the best role we can while we're here. We have a responsibility to do so, to ourselves—and to each other. Our soul seeks its highest expression in, and through, *us*.

Thank you for accompanying me into my multi-dimensional world. It's filled with one surprise after another, and the gifts are endless. It's my heartfelt desire, that in spite of this limited, linear mode of reaching you, the power of my *conscious intentions* sent forth in the flow will lift you to a new frequency on which you'll feel a new sense of hope, freedom and expansion.

May you be left with a new sense of excitement and a willingness to embrace the unseen and the unknown—so that you might come to see and sense so very much more!

Enjoy life in the flow!

Made in the USA
Middletown, DE
14 March 2021

34610681R00076